Anne Frank

Dit is een
foto, zoals
ik me zou
wensen, altijd zo
te zijn.
Dan had
ik nog wel een kans
om naar Holywood te
komen. Maar tegen-
woordig zie ik er
jammer genoeg meos-
tal anders uit.
Annefrank.
10 Oct. 1942
Zondag.

Anne Frank

Kem Knapp Sawyer

DK Publishing, Inc.

DK

LONDON, NEW YORK, MELBOURNE, MUNICH, AND DELHI

Designed for DK Publishing
by Mark Johnson Davies

Editor : Elizabeth Hester
Series Editor : Beth Sutinis
Editorial Assistant : Madeline Farbman
Art Director : Dirk Kaufman
Publisher : Chuck Lang
Creative Director : Tina Vaughan
Photo Research : Tracy Armstead
Production : Chris Avgherinos
DTP Designer : Milos Orlovic

First American Edition, 2004
Published in the United States
by DK Publishing, Inc.
375 Hudson St., New York, New York 10014

04 05 06 07 08 10 9 8 7 6 5 4 3 2 1

Copyright © 2004 DK Publishing, Inc.

A catalog record for this book is available
from the Library of Congress.

ISBN: 0-7566-0341-2 (PB)
ISBN: 0-7566-0490-7 (HC)

Color reproduction by GRB Editrice s.r.l., Italy
Printed and bound in China by
South China Printing Co., Ltd.

Jacket images: Border images from left to right: ©Maria Austria/MAI Amsterdam: a; ©ANNE FRANK–Fonds, Basel/Anne Frank House, Amsterdam/Getty Images: b; ©Aviodrome Aerial Photography, Lelystad, NL: c; ©ANNE FRANK–Fonds, Basel/Anne Frank House, Amsterdam/Getty Images: d; ©Maria Austria/MAI Amsterdam: e; ©ANNE FRANK–Fonds, Basel/Anne Frank House, Amsterdam/Getty Images: f. Front jacket, main image: ©AFP/Corbis. Spine: ©ANNE FRANK–Fonds, Basel/Anne Frank House, Amsterdam/Getty Images. Back jacket, main image: ©Maria Austria/MAI Amsterdam.

The quotations on p. 52 ("I want to write…") and on p. 67 ("In the twilight…") are from ANNE FRANK: THE DIARY OF A YOUNG GIRL by Anne Frank, translated by B.M. Mooyart-Doubleday, copyright 1952 by Otto H. Frank. Used by permission of Doubleday, a division of Random House, Inc. All other quotations from Anne Frank's diary are from THE DIARY OF A YOUNG GIRL: THE DEFINITIVE EDITION by Anne Frank. Otto H. Frank & Mirjam Pressler, Editors, translated by Susan Massotty, copyright © 1995 by Doubleday, a division of Random House, Inc. Used by permission of Doubleday, a division of Random House, Inc.

Discover more at
www.dk.com

Contents

chapter 1

The Diary of Anne Frank

Miep heard loud footsteps outside the office door. It was the Gestapo officers in their heavy boots. The men arrived without notice, revolvers drawn. Miep knew immediately they had not come to ask questions. They already had all the information they needed. They had come that morning to arrest her friends.

Miep Gies worked in the Amsterdam office of Opekta, a spice factory in the Netherlands. Most people thought she led an ordinary life, spending the day at her desk and then bicycling home in the evening. But the office at 263 Prinsengracht held a dangerous secret.

After Germany invaded Holland and life became unbearable for Jews, Miep was willing to risk everything to help her Jewish friends escape arrest. In the building where she worked, on the other side of the storeroom, a bookcase concealed several rooms, home now to eight Jews who lived in hiding. Miep helped make it possible for them to survive.

One of the people in hiding was Miep's

Between 1941 and 1944, the Dutch Gestapo arrested thousands of Jews in Amsterdam.

employer, Otto Frank. He had always been kind and considerate, and, when Otto revealed his plan to go into hiding and asked for her help, she had not hesitated. Miep helped the Franks move into the secret living quarters. Soon Otto's business partner, his family, and a dentist were also sharing the space. For two years, she had kept them safe from the Gestapo.

But now the day she'd feared had come. She followed the Gestapo's orders and waited—

This bookcase on the third floor of an Amsterdam office building swung open to reveal the living space of eight Jewish residents.

hoping they would not find the bookcase that blocked the door to the secret living quarters.

Minutes passed, but there was nothing she could do. When the Gestapo returned to use the telephone, Miep knew they must have found the bookcase and the hidden living quarters. There was no escape for her friends.

GESTAPO

The Gestapo, part of the Nazi party's Secret State Police, was charged with finding and arresting Jews.

Later she listened once again to the loud footsteps of the Gestapo. This time they were taking away the prisoners. A police truck was waiting for

Anne filled her diary with pictures and stories, and treated it as her best friend. Most entries began, "Dear Kitty."

them outside. Miep could hear the doors slam shut. The future her friends faced was grim. They were Jews, and most Jews, once arrested, never returned.

When evening came, Miep and Bep Voskuijl, another office worker, took one last look at the secret living quarters. Anxious not to be caught, they moved quickly and quietly.

They found the Franks' home in terrible disorder. The Gestapo had rummaged through everything, no doubt looking for money or jewelry. Clothes, papers, books were thrown here and there on the floor. One object caught Miep's eye: It was a diary, a small red, green, and beige checked book. Scattered on the floor next to the diary were two notebooks and hundreds of loose pages.

Miep and Bep bent down to pick up the tissue-thin sheets of paper. They recognized the handwriting on the pages. It belonged to Anne, the Franks' youngest daughter. They both knew Anne kept a diary, and that more than anything she wanted to become a writer. The Gestapo may have taken other valuables, but they had left behind what Anne treasured most.

Miep and Bep had to hurry. If the Gestapo returned, they too could be arrested.

Miep took the diary, the notebooks, and all the papers back to her desk. She opened her bottom drawer and placed them there. She would keep the diary safe for Anne, her lively young friend with the spirited temper and the brilliant smile.

The Holocaust

After Adolf Hitler rose to power in 1933, his political party, the Nationalist Socialist German Workers, or Nazis, discriminated against Jews and took away their freedom. Jews could not socialize with non-Jews, run their own businesses, or attend the schools of their choice. More injustice, suffering, and violence followed. The Nazis arrested great numbers of Jews and sent them to labor camps where many were killed. Between 1933 and 1945, the period known as the Holocaust, six million Jews died—including one million children.

2

Otto and Edith

Both Anne's parents, Otto Frank and Edith Holländer, were Jewish and born in Germany, yet in their youth they escaped the discrimination that many other Jews experienced. They came from well-to-do families and moved in social circles that included Jews and non-Jews. They spent pleasant childhoods in comfortable surroundings and were free to go to schools of their own choosing.

Growing up in Frankfurt, Otto rode horses, played the cello, and studied opera. As a young man he enjoyed a lavish lifestyle, regularly attending banquets and balls. While he was a student at the University of Heidelberg, a classmate persuaded him to sail to New York and take a job at his father's

The Charleston, a popular dance in the 1920s, symbolized the carefree mood of the decade.

company—Macy's department store. Otto spent two years working there and then returned in 1911 to Germany to work at a metal engineering company. Four years later, he was called to fight in World War I and became a lieutenant in the German army. At the end of the war, Otto took over the family banking business.

The coastal town of San Remo, Italy, was one of many stops on the Franks' honeymoon trip.

Edith was born in 1900 in Aachen, a German city close to the Dutch border. Her family, the Holländers, were more religious than Otto's family. They observed the Sabbath and attended the synagogue, where Edith's brother sang in the choir. Edith learned Hebrew, as well as English and French. But though she was studious, Edith also liked to have fun. She played tennis, went to fancy parties, danced the Charleston, and spent vacations at the beach.

Edith and Otto were married on May 12, 1925, Otto's thirty-sixth birthday. The couple stood under a *chuppah* canopy in a traditional Jewish wedding ceremony, which was performed in a synagogue in Aachen. Edith, then 25, wore a fashionable low-waisted white dress with a square neck, adorned with fresh flowers and a long, billowy veil. Otto, tall and distinguished, was dressed in an elegant black suit.

The newlyweds spent their honeymoon on the Mediterranean

coast in Italy. They settled in Frankfurt, moving into Otto's mother's house. Their first daughter was born on February 16, 1926, and they named her Margot Betti after Edith's sister Betti, who had died at the age of 16.

Edith holds one-day-old Anne in a Frankfurt hospital. Otto, who had spent the night at the hospital while Edith was in labor, took this photo.

Edith kept a detailed account of her daughter's progress in a baby book. She recorded the first step and the first tooth, every new food, and every new word. Otto became an enthusiastic photographer, snapping pictures of Margot's birthday celebrations, her first day of school, and visits with Edith's parents in Aachen.

When Margot was one and a half, the Franks moved into their own home, renting a large two-story apartment in a yellow house on the outskirts of Frankfurt. A birch tree shaded the yard, the perfect place for Margot to play. With only a few Jewish families living in the neighborhood, there was no synagogue nearby. Otto rarely attended services, but Edith often returned to the synagogue near her mother-in-law's house on holy days.

On June 12, 1929, Edith gave birth to Annelies Marie in the Frankfurt hospital. Otto telephoned home to report the good news to Margot and their housekeeper. A proud father, he took photographs of Edith smiling as her new baby snuggled close to her.

Margot, whose favorite pastimes had included playing store and giving her dolls a bath, now loved entertaining her baby sister. Edith and Otto pampered their two little girls, but they soon found that Anne was not always easy to please. From the beginning she was a difficult baby and hard to control. Whereas Margot always seemed contented and had started sleeping through the night when she was only a few months old, Anne fussed and craved attention. As a toddler, her curiosity was extraordinary; so was her stubbornness.

Once Anne learned to talk, she didn't want to stop. But both girls would sit spellbound whenever Otto, a gifted storyteller, told one of his tales about two invisible sisters, both named Paula, one good, and the other bad. Even as the girls grew older, the two Paulas never lost their appeal. Anne always kept a special place in her heart for her father's stories.

Margot and Anne were devoted sisters, though very different; Margot was calm and quiet, while Anne could be wild and willful.

chapter 3

Leaving Germany

In the early 1930s, as the Nazi party gained power, anti-semitism, or discrimination against Jews, increased. Life was becoming more difficult for Jews in Frankfurt and throughout Germany. The Franks' landlord, a Nazi sympathizer, refused to continue renting to Jews. Otto and Edith found a new home in a different neighborhood, but there was still no end to the problems they faced: The 1929 stockmarket crash in the United States had caused problems for Otto's business, and by 1932 his bank had failed.

On January 30, 1933, Adolf Hitler was appointed chancellor of Germany, and in Berlin a huge torch-lit parade was held in celebration. When the Franks heard the announcement on the radio, they knew the situation in Germany would become even harder for Jews. Many of their non-Jewish friends had already stopped visiting them. Then a new law was passed that affected Margot. This law required

Adolf Hitler, leader of the Nazi party, insisted that the Jews were the cause of Germany's troubles.

The Weimar Republic

In 1919, the defeat of Germany in World War I brought the formation of a new democratic government, called the Weimar Republic. By the terms of the peace treaty, Germany had to surrender land, reduce its army, and pay reparations—huge sums of money—to the victorious nations. The situation led to an economic depression and high unemployment. Many Jews left Germany—63,000 had emigrated by 1933.

Signs reading JEWS ARE NOT WANTED IN THIS PLACE were posted on the streets.

Jewish children to sit apart from non-Jews in the classroom. It angered Edith and Otto to think their daughter would be treated this way.

That April the Nazis staged a boycott of Jewish businesses. They put up signs that read DON'T BUY FROM JEWS and painted the yellow Star of David, the symbol of Judaism, on the windows of shops owned by Jews, to drive customers away. New laws made it even more difficult for Jews to own a business or work in one. On May 10, 1933, university students who supported the Nazis organized book burnings in 30 cities and towns. They destroyed 25,000 books considered

Nazi Propaganda

Adolf Hitler named Dr. Joseph Goebbels to head the Nazi National Ministry for Public Enlightenment and Propaganda. Goebbels and his ministry set out to promote Hitler and increase fierce anti-Semitism. The Nazis rewrote textbooks, distributed cartoons making fun of Jews, and posted flyers with anti-Jewish decrees. They censored news, literature, and art that supported Jews or criticized Nazis.

"un-German," including works by famous Jewish authors such as Albert Einstein and Sigmund Freud. Then came the pogroms: The Nazis attacked Jews and vandalized their shops. They arrested Jews by the thousands and sent them to prison or forced labor camps.

With the political climate changing so drastically, the Franks decided they must leave their native country. Otto's brother-in-law worked in Switzerland for Opekta, a company that made pectin, a product used in making jams. He agreed to loan Otto the money to open an Opekta office in Amsterdam. In August 1933, Otto left for Amsterdam to start his new business while the children went to Aachen to stay with their grandmother.

Edith traveled back and forth between Aachen and Amsterdam. After several months, she and Otto found an apartment at 37 Merwedeplein, in a section

> **POGROM**
>
> A pogrom is an organized attack against a minority group.

of Amsterdam where many German Jews had moved. Their apartment, on the third floor of the building, was pleasant and comfortable, but not as large as their home in Frankfurt. The tan-brick, modern apartment complex surrounded a small plaza where the children could play. Margot joined her parents in December so that she would be ready to start school in January. Anne stayed with her

The Franks found a comfortable new home in the Merwedeplein apartment complex in Amsterdam. They often walked across the square to visit with neighbors.

grandmother a little longer and did not arrive in Amsterdam until February 16, 1934, Margot's eighth birthday.

The Franks adjusted well to the move and made new friends. Anne had to walk only a few blocks to school. Like Margot, she quickly learned Dutch. The two girls played outside with the many neighborhood children. On Friday evenings, the family enjoyed visiting the Goslars, who lived at 31 Merwedeplein. They observed the Sabbath together, listening to Hans Goslar recite the *kiddush*, the traditional Jewish blessing, before starting their meal. It seemed the decision to move to Amsterdam had been a wise one.

chapter 4

"I Don't Dare Do Anything Anymore"

Over the years, the Franks and the Goslars became very good friends. They always looked forward to spending holidays together, whether it was observing Passover or eating doughnuts at midnight on New Year's Eve.

After school and on Sundays, Anne, the Goslars' daughter Hanneli, and Sanne Ledermann, who also lived on the Merwedeplein, were inseparable. Since Hanneli and Sanne were both shy and quiet, Anne became the leader of their tight-knit group. Anne was quick to organize hopscotch, Ping-Pong, or other games. Sometimes the girls got into trouble, but they almost always had fun. One of their favorite pranks was to throw water on people from the apartment building windows.

Anne (right), six years old, plays with her friend Sanne Ledermann (left) outside the Franks' apartment in Amsterdam.

When the weather permitted, Anne and her friends sunbathed on the roof of the Franks' apartment building. On rainy afternoons, they enjoyed going to the Franks' for lemonade and the rolls with cream cheese that Edith liked to fix. If Otto was there, he would tell jokes and make them laugh.

Anne often insisted on having her way. Hanneli's mother would say, "God knows everything, but Anne knows everything better."

Montessori Schools

Dr. Maria Montessori opened the first Montessori school in Rome in 1907. Her methods encouraged students to progress at their own pace. This new educational system was outlawed in Germany, but became popular in Amsterdam in the 1930s, especially with immigrant children who did not know Dutch.

But Anne was also a very considerate child. She loved taking care of babies and was always eager to push Hanneli's little sister in the baby carriage. She was fond of older people and was often seen helping an elderly neighbor cross the street. And Anne always looked forward to her grandmother's visits.

The Montessori school Anne attended was less than a 10-minute walk from her home. She liked school and, from an early age, excelled in writing and history. Yet she found it difficult to keep still no matter how hard she tried. While Margot excelled in all subjects, Anne never did well in math.

She spent many nights practicing her multiplication tables with her father.

Anne was very thin and had difficulty gaining weight. She frequently had to miss school due to illness. She loved ice skating and gymnastics, but because of her poor health, she was not allowed to participate in more rigorous sports.

Although Edith occasionally felt homesick, the Franks enjoyed their first five years in Amsterdam. They found less discrimination and lived with less fear. They socialized freely with Jews and non-Jews. Otto could hire whomever he pleased in his business, and

Anne and her father (center) join other guests on their way to the city hall in Amsterdam where Miep Santrouschitz and Jan Gies were to be married. The next day, Otto held a party for the newlyweds at his office.

Margot and Anne's schools were open to children of all religions.

But in Germany, the situation for Jews had only grown more dangerous. On November 9, 1938, the night that later came to be known as Kristallnacht, Nazi rioters in Aachen burned a synagogue and Jewish homes. Edith's brother Walter was arrested along with 247 men from Aachen and sent to a concentration camp.

On Saturday afternoons, the Franks would invite several of their friends,

Kristallnacht

On November 9, 1938, the Nazis attacked Jewish businesses, burned more than one thousand synagogues, and vandalized schools, cemeteries, and homes throughout Germany and Austria. Joseph Goebbels, the minister for Public Enlightenment and Propaganda, secretly organized the attacks. The next morning, the Gestapo arrested 30,000 Jews.

mostly German Jewish refugees, to come by the apartment for coffee and cake. They'd discuss politics and the lives they had left behind. From week to week the world around them was quickly changing, and their future was becoming more and more uncertain. The relatively pleasant life they led would not last forever.

Hitler and the German army invaded Poland on September 1, 1939. Great Britain and France declared war on Germany. The Second World War had begun. On May 10, 1940, German troops invaded the Netherlands. After five days of fighting, the Netherlands surrendered. The German takeover marked a turning point for Anne. She wrote in her diary, "After May 1940 the good times were few and far between."

Anne had just turned 11 when the Germans enforced harsh anti-Jewish decrees in Amsterdam. Jews were not allowed to go to parks, swimming pools, theaters, or ice-skating rinks—a big disappointment for Anne. They had to do their shopping between 3:00 and 5:00 PM, and they could not be on the street after 8:00 PM. All Jews were forced to register and wear a yellow star as a means of identification.

The Star of David is a symbol of Judaism. The Nazis required all Jews to wear a yellow star on their clothing.

The Germans also required all Dutch citizens to carry identity cards with passport photos and fingerprints. They stamped a "J" on the cards belonging to Jews.

Meanwhile the Dutch Nazi party (NSB) was gaining in both numbers and importance. The NSB destroyed property and put up signs that read NO JEWS ALLOWED. On February 22, 1941, they started the first roundup of the Jews in Amsterdam, arresting 425 Jewish men in two days.

Jews were also required to attend Jewish schools. Anne and her Jewish friends had to transfer to the Jewish Lyceum when Anne was in seventh grade. No longer allowed to use the streetcar or ride a bike, they walked 40 minutes each way.

Math was still Anne's most challenging subject, and it was hard for her to concentrate in class. Mr. Keesing, her math teacher, punished her for talking too much by assigning an essay to be titled "A Chatterbox." Anne won him over with her clever writing. In her diary Anne wrote that she worked hard to get better grades, but that her parents never worried about her report cards. They wanted her to be happy and healthy and not talk back.

Anne liked to sunbathe on the roof of the Franks' apartment building.

At her new school Anne became good friends with Jacqueline van Maarsen, who also lived on the Merwedeplein. Jacqueline helped Anne with her math homework. They played Monopoly, read the same books, spent the night at each other's house, and went to the Oasis, a Jewish ice-cream parlor near their home.

Anne and her friends loved to look at fashion magazines and collect pictures of movie stars. Anne often put on skits and enjoyed being the center of attention. She was also popular with the boys in her class. Several liked her, and an older boy, Hello Silberberg, sometimes brought her cake and candy.

1942 was in many ways a difficult year for Anne. She had been forced to change schools, and her freedom had become

On June 12, 1939, Anne (second from the left) celebrated her tenth birthday with her friends, including Sanne (third from the left) and Hanneli (fourth from the left).

more restricted. In January 1942, Edith's mother, Rosa Holländer, who had come to live with the Franks, died of cancer and Anne felt the loss deeply.

On Friday, June 12, Anne turned 13. Edith and Otto were determined to mark the occasion in a special way. There was one present Anne wanted most of all—the red-checked diary she'd seen at the bookshop around the corner on Waal Street. Otto bought the diary for her, and Anne was allowed to open it before she went to school. As a special treat, Edith made a delicious strawberry tart.

Anne's birthday party was planned for that Sunday. She invited Hanneli, Sanne, Jacqueline, and other friends to come watch *The Lighthouse Keeper*, a movie starring the heroic dog Rin Tin Tin. Since Jews could no longer go to the movie theater, the Franks would show the movie in their own home. Anne couldn't wait.

The party was a big success—just as Edith and Otto had hoped. They worked hard to make it possible for Margot and Anne to lead as normal a life as possible, and wanted to protect their children from the suffering of the Jews and the horrors of the war. "My wife and I did our best not to show our sorrows," Otto explained later. They took great satisfaction in knowing that Anne had enjoyed her party.

But they could not shield their daughters forever from the terrible changes brought about by the Nazis. As Anne's friend Jacqueline said, "I don't dare do anything anymore 'cause I'm afraid it's not allowed."

chapter **5**

A Secret Plan

A few weeks after Anne's thirteenth birthday, Otto took Anne for a walk on the Merwedeplein outside their apartment. What he told her that day shocked and scared her. It would not be safe for their family to stay in their apartment, he said. In order to escape the "clutches" of the Germans, they would have to go into hiding. For more than a year, he and Edith had been preparing for the move. The plan was secret, and Otto did not want to reveal many details. He didn't want Anne and Margot to worry.

The Franks were only one of many families to go into hiding. That summer the Germans had sent out call-up notices to Jews in Amsterdam telling them to report to transit camps. If they refused to go, they would be arrested. Jews who had not already fled the Netherlands looked for safe places to hide in order to avoid deportation to the camps.

Because Jews needed to be registered with the government and always had to carry identity cards, it was difficult for them to go unnoticed. Hiding from the authorities would be difficult for the Jews, and those who helped them were also in danger. People caught helping a Jew hide or escape could also be arrested.

CALL-UP

During a call-up, Jews were required to report to a central office and then sent to labor camps.

Some Jews, like the family of Anne's friend Jacqueline van Maarsen, did whatever they could to avoid this classification, such as producing documents to prove the existence of non-Jewish grandparents. Jacqueline's mother, who had been born a Catholic and later converted to Judaism, went to great trouble to locate baptismal records of her four grandparents. The van Maarsens were taken off the deportation list and were allowed to remove their Jewish stars. Jacqueline withdrew from the Jewish Lyceum and remained safe in Amsterdam during the war.

Deportation

Margot was one of one thousand Jews to receive call-up notices on July 5, 1942. Nine days later the Nazis deported the first group of Jews to Westerbork, a transit camp in northern Holland. From there the Jews were sent to concentration camps in Germany and Poland. Of the 140,000 Jews living in the Netherlands during the Holocaust, 107,000 were deported to concentration camps. Only 5,500 returned alive from the camps.

But for the Franks, there was no escape from their Jewish heritage. On Sunday, July 5, 1942, Anne was spending the afternoon on the balcony, enjoying the sunshine and reading a book. She was expecting her friend Hello to drop by. The doorbell to the Franks' apartment rang. Anne did not hear the bell, and Edith answered the door.

A little while later Anne looked up from her book and saw Margot standing in the doorway. Margot, usually so calm, was very upset. She whispered to Anne that the postman had brought a registered letter with a call-up notice. Otto was being sent to a work camp.

Otto knew nothing about the call-up. He was visiting friends at the Jewish hospital and would not be back until later that evening. Their mother had gone to see Mr. van Pels, Otto's business partner and friend, to ask his advice.

The doorbell rang again. Anne thought it must be Hello and wanted to answer it, but Margot stopped her. Under no circumstances were they to answer the door. Then the sisters heard voices. Edith had returned with Mr. van Pels and was downstairs talking to Hello. She told Hello this was not a good time to visit. Then she and Mr. van Pels came upstairs.

Edith explained to the girls that they would have to go into hiding sooner than planned.

The van Pels family would join them later. Margot and Anne were stunned. For once Anne could hardly speak. Edith asked the girls to start packing.

Margot and Anne went back to their bedroom, and Anne put her diary, curlers, handkerchiefs, schoolbooks, a comb, and old letters into a schoolbag. Everything was happening so quickly. There was so much Anne didn't know.

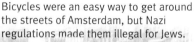

Bicycles were an easy way to get around the streets of Amsterdam, but Nazi regulations made them illegal for Jews.

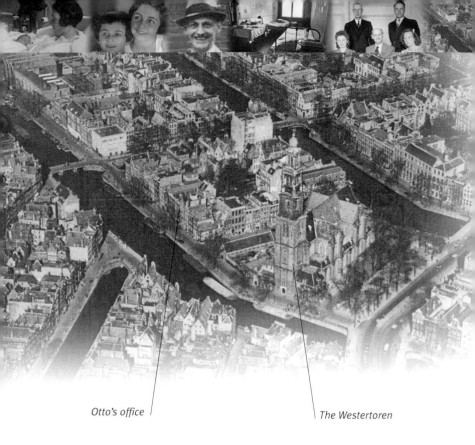

Otto's office

The Westertoren

Where were they going? How long would they have to stay? She didn't like not getting to say good-bye to her friends and she didn't want to leave Moortje, her cat, behind.

Otto Frank's company was located on the Prinsengracht, one of Amsterdam's many canals.

Then Margot told her the call-up was not for their father, but for Margot. She was due to report in nine days to the Gestapo's Central Office. She would be taken from there to the transit camp at Westerbork. Anne started to cry. She could not bear to think of her sister, only 16 years old, being sent off on her own to a work camp.

At 5:00 in the afternoon, Otto returned. Mr. van Pels went

to tell Miep and her husband, Jan Gies, that the Franks were going into hiding right away. He asked them if they could collect a few things from the Franks' apartment to bring to them later. The news was unexpected, but Miep and Jan immediately put on their raincoats and hurried to the Merwedeplein. Edith gave them bags of clothes to hide under their raincoats. They left quickly so they would have time to make a second trip that evening.

Mr. Goldschmidt, who rented a room from the Franks, stopped to visit with the family. The Franks tried hard not to let him know what was going on. They kept hoping he'd leave them alone, but he didn't go to bed until 10:00. Miep and Jan returned later that night and once again stuffed their pockets and carried out bags of clothes and books. They would leave the bags in their apartment temporarily and bring them to the hiding place later.

That night Anne fell asleep in her own bed for the last time. Early the next morning, at 5:30, Edith woke Margot and Anne. She told them to wear as many layers as possible. They could not carry any large bags or suitcases, for that would only raise suspicion. Anne wrote in her diary that the four of them wore so many clothes they looked as if they "were going off to spend the night in a refrigerator."

Miep arrived in the rain at 7:30 AM to pick up Margot. The two of them were going to ride bikes to the hiding place. (Although Jews had been ordered to hand in their bicycles, Margot had kept hers hidden.) Miep assured Edith and Otto that the rain would keep the police off the streets. She and Margot would be safe.

Margot was not wearing her yellow star. As long as no one stopped them, she and Miep would look like two young women on their way to work. They bicycled in the rain through the busy streets, over bridges, and then onto Prinsengracht and along the canal to Otto's office. Otto and his partner Mr. van Pels had set up their business in a 300-year-old red brick building. It was five stories tall, with large windows that opened onto a narrow cobblestone street bordering the canal. A few doors away, bells from the Westertoren, the church clock tower, chimed every quarter hour.

As soon as they arrived at the office, Miep led Margot through the empty building and then upstairs. She opened the door to the hiding place. Margot entered alone, and

Johannes Kleiman

Otto Frank's (center) four employees helped the Franks prepare their secret hiding place.

Victor Kugler

Bep Voskuijl

Miep Gies

Miep returned downstairs. She needed to be at her desk when the others came in to work.

Anne and her parents watched Miep and Margot ride off on their bikes. Then they closed the door to their apartment for the last time and started the long walk across town to Otto's office. Otto and Edith explained to Anne that they would be living in the rooms connected to the back of Otto's office. None of the rooms was visible from the street. Only a few people knew of the plan—Miep and her husband Jan, and three others who worked in the office: Bep Voskuijl, Victor Kugler, and Johannes Kleiman. Mr. Kugler and Mr. Kleiman had worked hard to furnish the hiding place.

By the time Anne and her parents reached the office, the rain had soaked through their many layers of clothes. Miep met them and accompanied them up the stairs and along a corridor where no one could see them, and then to the hiding place. What a relief to see that Margot was safe!

Anne looked around at the small rooms. They were crowded with furniture and the belongings the Franks and van Pelses had accumulated with help from their friends. No wonder it had taken more than six months to prepare the hiding place! Boxes and bags were filled to the brim with linens, clothing, bedding, and cooking utensils.

The events of the last 24 hours were more than Edith and Margot could handle. They collapsed on their beds. But Otto and Anne couldn't rest. They had to start unpacking and fixing up their new home.

chapter 6

Inside the Hidden Annex

The Franks told none of their friends they were going into hiding. They left behind a note with an address in Maastricht, a city to the south, scribbled on it. They wanted Mr. Goldschmidt to find the note and tell their friends. Since most everyone knew Otto had family in Switzerland, they would assume the Franks had gone there, stopping in Maastricht along the way.

The front of the building at 263 Prinsengracht held the Opekta offices. In July 1942, the Franks moved into the rear of the building above the warehouse.

The plan worked. On Monday, after the Franks departed, Hanneli went by the Franks' apartment to see if she could borrow a cooking scale for her mother. Mr. Goldschmidt told Hanneli that the family had left hastily and must be on their way to Switzerland. The news took Hanneli by surprise. Anne was the first of her friends to disappear without warning.

Anne's friend Jacqueline had called Anne while the family was packing, but Anne had said nothing about leaving. Jacqueline and

Hanneli both visited the apartment later to find more information. They couldn't believe all that Anne had left behind—a favorite pair of shoes, all her books and games. Little was missing, only the diary she'd received as a birthday present and her movie star pictures.

Hello also came by the apartment to see Anne. He rang the bell several times, but no one ever answered the door. He finally decided that the Franks must have found a way to escape.

Little did Anne's friends know that the Franks were now hiding on the other

Hidden Children

Of the 140,000 Jews living in the Netherlands, 25,000 went into hiding. Parents often made the painful decision to send away their children to live with Christian families or in convents or orphanages. Wilhelmina Salters-Kloppenburg (shown here) and her husband took a Jewish child, Elizabeth Reiss, into their home. They cut and dyed her hair to conceal her identity and sent her to a Catholic school.

side of the city. Within a few days, they had unpacked their belongings and made the Secret Annex look more like a home. They arranged the furniture, scrubbed the floors, and sewed curtains for the windows.

Anne glued her pictures of movie stars and royal families on the walls of the little room she and

ANNEX

An annex is an extra space or building added onto a main structure.

Margot shared. It was long and narrow, with mustard yellow wallpaper that was starting to peel. A bed, a cot, and a desk filled the room so there was hardly room to walk. Anne had to put a chair at the end of the cot to make it long enough to sleep on. A green door led to the large bathroom with a sink and toilet, and another door opened onto her parents' small bedroom.

On July 13, one week after the Franks moved into the secret annex, the van Pels family arrived. Auguste carried her chamberpot inside a hatbox, Hermann brought a

Mr. and Mrs. van Pelses' room

Attic

Otto and Edith's room

Front of house

Anne and Margot's room

Bookcase entrance

The secret annex housed the Franks and Hermann, Auguste, and Peter van Pels. The residents found little privacy in the cramped living space.

Staircase to annex

36

collapsible tea table, and Peter, their 16-year-old son, smuggled in his cat, Mousche. The parents settled into the largest room, on the floor above the Franks. With a table, a wood stove, and a sink, it would also serve as a living room and kitchen for the two families. Peter's room was barely big enough for a bed. A wobbly ladder led to the attic where the families could keep food supplies and hang the laundry to dry.

The Franks and the van Pelses had to get used to living quarters with no bathtub and no hot water. At night or on weekends, when the office was empty, they carried a washtub downstairs where they would find hot water. Each one found a favorite spot to bathe—Otto in his old office, Edith in the downstairs kitchen, Margot in the front office, and Anne in the office bathroom.

Every morning, before the other workers arrived at the office, Miep came upstairs to get a shopping list from Edith and Mrs. van Pels. Anne would rush to her side and ask questions. "Hello Miep, what's the news?" she'd say. She wanted to know everything that was happening. Then, during work hours, the residents had to stay very quiet so that no one in the office below could hear a sound. They could not wear

Anne pasted pictures and postcards on the walls of the room she shared with Margot to make it feel more like home.

shoes, talk in a loud voice, or flush the toilet.

Both families looked forward to dinnertime, when they could be themselves, laugh, and tell jokes. On July 18, they invited Miep and Jan for dinner to celebrate their helpers' first wedding anniversary. Anne even typed a special menu. It included "Bouillon a la Hunzestraat," named for the street where the Gieses lived, and "Roast beef Scholte," in honor of their butcher. There were also two salads, potatoes, and raspberry juice with sugar and cinnamon to accompany the "coffee with sugar, cream, and various surprises."

Inside the annex, Anne felt safe. But outside, the *razias*, or roundups of Jews, increased. On August 6, 1942, later known as Black Thursday, Jews in Amsterdam were arrested at gunpoint, beaten, and taken away.

For their own security, Otto wanted to hide the door to the annex. The residents and helpers decided they could trust Bep's father, Johan Voskuijl, the warehouse manager, with their secret and asked for his help.

A large bookcase concealed the entrance to the hiding place. The bookcase could swing open to let the helpers in and out.

Mr. Voskuijl decided to construct a bookcase that would swing to the side when the door was in use. No one would be the least suspicious.

The van Pelses' bedroom also served as the living room, dining room, and kitchen for all the residents.

As the weeks passed, the excitement of being in a new place faded. Anne grew weary of the quiet. She longed for a change, and begged Miep and Jan to spend the night in the annex. When Miep said yes, Anne was delighted. Edith was pleased because she knew how happy this would make Anne.

On the appointed night, Miep and Jan came for dinner and were treated like royalty. They talked for a long time over dessert. Then Anne and Margot went to sleep in their parents' room so that Miep and Jan could have their room.

Later, Miep lay in bed with blankets piled on top of her, but she could not sleep. Spending the night in the secret annex was not what she expected. She could hear each little sound—a bed creaking, a slipper dropping, Mr. van Pels coughing from the room above. Every 15 minutes she listened to the chiming of the Westertoren bells.

Miep was frightened. The thought of what it must be like to be a Jew in hiding kept her awake all night.

chapter 7

Routine, Risk, and Rations

"Miep, where seven can eat, eight people can eat as well," Otto told Miep. Miep had asked the people in hiding if they would consider allowing her dentist, Fritz Pfeffer, to move in. Dr. Pfeffer, a Jew, had emigrated from Germany and was now in need of a safe hiding place.

After discussing the matter with each other, the Franks and the van Pelses agreed to take in Dr. Pfeffer. Margot would have to move into her parents' room, and Anne would share her room with

The arrival of German trucks often signaled a roundup. The Gestapo arrested Jews in their homes and sent them to concentration camps.

Dr. Pfeffer. Anne didn't think of the inconveniences. She liked the excitement of adding a new person to their secret annex. She also understood that if Dr. Pfeffer remained on the outside he would be arrested and sent to a concentration camp.

> *"Singing: Only softly, and after 6:00."*
>
> Anne Frank's "Guide to the Secret Annex"

Dr. Pfeffer moved into the hiding place on November 16, 1942. Anne wrote a "Guide to the Secret Annex" for the new arrival, containing a list of rules and a detailed schedule: Regular sleeping hours were from 10:00 PM to 7:30 AM (10:15 AM on Sundays), but residents were also required "to observe rest hours during the daytime when instructed to do so by the Management." Of course no activities were allowed outside the house. Singing was allowed, but "only softly, and after 6:00 PM." The restrictions in the annex were annoying, but Anne had been quick to make the best of the situation, and she expected Dr. Pfeffer to do the same.

Dr. Pfeffer brought news of their friends, many of whom had been arrested. The Gestapo were stopping at every house to search for Jews. Anne wrote in her diary that she felt lucky to be safe but was still frightened to think of friends who were "now at the mercy of the cruelest monsters ever to stalk the earth. And all because they're Jews."

In her diary Anne wrote about the adjustments the residents made to adapt to a new routine. She reported that the annex was well stocked with 100 cans of food and 300 pounds of beans. Mr. van Pels, who had once worked in the meat business, made sausages for the residents. Mrs. van Pels took charge of most of the cooking, while Edith oversaw the cleaning. Potatoes were plentiful, so they were served at almost every meal. All the residents had to help with the potato peeling.

Anne awoke every morning at 6:45 to the sound of the van Pelses' alarm clock. Mr. van Pels used the bathroom and was followed by Dr. Pfeffer. Anne didn't get out of bed until 7:15. By 8:30, all the residents were finished dressing and eating. They needed to remain as still as possible, tiptoeing and never talking above a whisper so that the employees downstairs wouldn't hear them. Mornings were spent reading or working quietly. Anne, Margot, and Peter studied the subjects they would have been taking in school.

As soon as the employees left for lunch, Bep came upstairs to tell the residents they were free to move around. She brought with her the milk that had been delivered to the office. One or two of the other helpers might also join them for lunch. Then in the afternoon the residents once again took up their silent activities. Otto insisted that the young

people stick to a rigid study schedule and often reminded them of his motto: "Work and Hope."

At the end of the day Bep came up to the secret annex to let the residents know the employees had gone home. Now the residents could walk around or go downstairs. Peter fetched the bread from the warehouse while Otto and Mr. van Pels worked in the office, attending to Mr. Kugler and Mr. Kleiman's questions about the company business. Dr. Pfeffer wrote letters to his fiancée, a Christian who did not have to go into hiding. Margot and Anne helped with some of the filing or bookkeeping that Miep and Bep had left for them. Mrs. van Pels and Edith took charge of the dinner preparations.

The residents often lingered over dinner, talking about whatever news they'd heard from the helpers. Then, at 9:00, they started their preparations for bed. They took turns using the bathroom, each at a pre-arranged time. They unfolded blankets and pulled out beds. Anne turned off her light at 10:00 but always awoke at 11:30 when she heard Dr. Pfeffer enter the room. (After dinner, he worked or read in the downstairs office.)

Bep worked as Miep's assistant in the office and also helped the residents in the Secret Annex by bringing food and supplies.

Anne was sometimes kept awake by the sound of Dr. Pfeffer rearranging his pillows. At other times she was awakened by the sound of sirens, air raid warnings, planes flying overhead, and gunfire, frequent reminders of the war that surrounded them. She'd grab her pillow and run into her parents' bedroom. Sometimes it seemed the dark night would last forever.

During the war, the Dutch were allowed to buy only limited amounts of food, using ration coupons issued by the government. Miep's husband Jan obtained extra coupons through his connections with the Dutch Resistance, who knew that he was helping Jews in hiding. Miep used the ration coupons to do most of the shopping. She also bought some food on the black market.

The butcher, a friend of Mr. van Pels who knew of Miep's secret mission, often added extra meat to her order. The grocer who sold fruits and vegetables realized Miep must be shopping for others besides herself and her husband. He never asked any questions, but he

Ration books like these kept track of how many portions of food each citizen was allowed. Since Jews in hiding could not receive rations officially, they relied on their helpers to find other ways of procuring supplies.

helped out by putting produce aside for her. The baker, one of Mr. Kleiman's friends, delivered bread to the office, much of it provided on credit, to be paid for after the war. But even with help from friends Miep had to work hard to find enough food.

Of course none of the residents could ever go outside. They looked forward to any change in the routine. Jan borrowed books from Como's, a bookshop and lending library, and Miep brought them to the residents every Saturday. Mr. Kugler always remembered to pick up the latest *Cinema and Theater* magazine for Anne. Miep once bought

The radio was a crucial link to news of the war—especially through non-German stations such as the BBC.

Anne a second-hand pair of suede high heels, a perfect present for a girl who loved fancy clothes. Both Miep and Bep kept Anne and Margot well supplied with paper. The helpers never forgot a birthday, and they always found enough money to buy a small present, flowers, cake, or special dessert.

The helpers' cheerfulness and loyalty did not go unnoticed. Mrs. van Pels pulled Miep aside on her birthday to give her an antique ring as a present. Miep knew if she sold the ring, the money could be used for food, but Mrs. van Pels insisted Miep keep it for herself.

Anne not only recognized the helpers' generous spirit, but she knew, too, that they were risking their lives to make it possible for the residents of the Secret Annex to survive. One careless mistake could lead not only to the capture of the residents but also to the helpers' arrest.

The news broadcast on the radio made them all well aware of the danger they faced. Every afternoon, at 1:00, while the office was closed for lunch, the residents went downstairs to the office to listen to the news from the BBC, the British Broadcasting Corporation. They returned at 7:00, after the employees had left, for another round of news. They also sometimes listened to Radio Orange, the Dutch government station that was broadcast out of London. The Germans had placed a ban on these stations, but people ignored the ban and tuned in secretly. The residents heard that the Russians had defeated the Germans at Stalingrad in February 1943. But they also knew that Jews continued to be arrested and that they were being deported to concentration camps.

Although many non-Jews were appalled and angered by what they saw during the Nazi takeover, they remained silent and did nothing. Some acted this way out of fear.

Allied forces fought to liberate Nazi-occupied Europe.

The Nazis had threatened to impose severe penalties on those who tried to assist the Jews. They too could be sent to work camps. Others simply ignored or refused to believe what was happening around them.

But there were also those, like Miep and Jan Gies, Bep, Mr. Kugler, and Mr. Kleiman, who did what they could to help the Jews survive. Some provided clothing, food, or money. Others took Jews into their own homes for a few days or several months. (Miep and Jan not only helped their friends in the annex, but also hid a young university student in their home.)

On April 29, 1943, the Germans announced that they would send 300,000 Dutch soldiers as prisoners of war to labor camps in Germany. Workers in Dutch factories responded by going on strike. Within three

The Nazis confiscated radios in their effort to control the kind of information reaching citizens of the countries they had conquered.

days, the Germans killed 175 strikers. The Germans ordered the Dutch to turn in their radios so they would be cut off from any communication from the Allies. Otto's large cabinet radio was taken from the office in July, but Mr. Kleiman managed to smuggle a small radio into the Secret Annex so that the residents could still maintain their link to the outside world.

Life for the residents was filled with fear. They heard noises at night, some real and some imagined. Living in tight quarters became more difficult. And the food that once seemed abundant was harder to come by.

Rescuers and Resisters

Some people took great risks to protect their homeland and their fellow citizens from the Nazis. Many provided clothing, food, or money. Others took Jews into their own homes—often for a few days, but some for months or years. They forged documents, such as birth certificates, to help Jews get out of danger, plotted ways for them to escape, and did what they could to help the Jews survive.

No matter how bad living in the annex seemed, Anne knew it was better than the alternative. Besides, it was only temporary. The end of the war would come soon, and with it the freedom that made the waiting all worthwhile.

8

The Writer

Anne couldn't wait for the war to end so she could go back to school. She wanted to see her friends and attend regular classes. Every day she spent several hours studying so she would be prepared. She tried to keep up with all 12 of the courses she had started at the Lyceum, including geometry, history, geography, art history, biology, Dutch, French, English, and German.

Anne especially loved history, even though some of the reading could be slow going. She was usually a fast reader, but she found it took her five days to read 50 pages of the 598-page biography of Emperor Charles V, ruler of the Netherlands, Spain, and Germany in the sixteenth century. Her most difficult subject was math. Otto tried to help her, but even he couldn't solve the toughest problems. For those, they went to Margot.

What Were They Reading?

Everyone in the annex kept busy with reading and studying. Mrs. van Pels and Edith were both taking correspondence courses in English. Mrs. van Pels read biographies, while Edith read everything except detective stories. Mr. van Pels was fond of detective stories and would also read from the encyclopedia. Otto studied Latin and, with the help of a dictionary, was reading novels by Charles Dickens. Dr. Pfeffer was trying to teach himself English, Spanish, and Dutch, but none of these languages came easily to him.

Margot studied the same subjects as Anne at a more advanced level, as well as trigonometry, physics, and chemistry. She taught herself most of her courses, but she also used Bep's name to register for a correspondence class in Latin. She relied on Bep to send the completed lessons to a teacher who corrected them and then returned them by mail.

Anne had always liked to read. Living in the annex, she found time to read a great variety of books, novels, adventure stories, biographies, and stories from the Bible. She often grew fond of characters in books; many of them she considered her friends. One of her very favorite books she read while in hiding was a Greek and Roman mythology book she received for her fourteenth birthday. Although no one in the annex read contemporary German books, Otto wanted Anne to become familiar with the classics. He insisted she listen as he read aloud

Anne confided her deepest secrets In her dlary, and, as she wrote, she felt her sorrows disappear.

plays by Goethe and Schiller. Edith gave her a German prayer book and urged her to read it.

"When I write I can shake off all my cares."

Anne Frank

Peter, Margot, and Anne would often read together in Anne's room or in the attic. At first Anne was not allowed to read some of the books Margot and Peter were reading. Anne was furious. She couldn't believe her parents were so unreasonable. Finally they gave in and let her read what she pleased.

Anne took great pleasure in her favorite hobby: working on the family trees of European royalty. She also enjoyed tracing her own family roots, with Otto's help. But what Anne liked most was writing in her diary. In school, Anne had made many friends, yet she always wanted "one true friend." Her diary was to become that one true friend.

Anne shared her desk with Dr. Pfeffer, who wrote letters to his fiancée here. Anne could only use the desk at scheduled times.

"I want to write," she said, "but more than that, I want to bring out all kinds of things that lie buried deep in my heart." She would reveal her most intimate feelings, the pain of confinement, and her desperate longing to once again be allowed outside.

Anne not only confided in her diary, but she also wrote short stories—memories from childhood and what Anne called "amusing sketches" of people in the annex. The residents all loved listening to Anne's descriptions of life in the Secret Annex and were always very attentive. Anne was witty and honest in her writing and often made her audience burst out laughing.

Orphans, fairies, elves, a granny who became a guardian angel, and a bear named Blurry appeared as characters in Anne's stories. Several of these stories were fables in which characters choose between right and wrong. They talked about the beauty of nature and discussed the meaning of life. One character believed that nature—the sun and blue sky—helps cure people of despair and brings them closer to God. Another learned that people need to laugh and weep, but each "at the right time."

It was not always easy to find a private area in which to write and work. Dr. Pfeffer and Anne had to share the one desk in their room, but Anne was only permitted to use the desk between 2:30 and 4:00 PM, while Dr. Pfeffer was napping. This bothered Anne so much that she decided to talk to Dr. Pfeffer. She told him she wanted more time to use the desk and asked for additional hours two afternoons a week. The discussion started calmly, but then Anne and Dr. Pfeffer both lost their tempers. They argued in loud, angry voices. Neither one would give in. Only after Otto spoke up for Anne did Dr. Pfeffer finally agree to let Anne use the desk until 5:30 PM two afternoons a week.

While she was writing Anne's concentration was intense. She liked to be allowed to write without interruptions. When Miep came up to the annex one afternoon to visit, she found Anne at her desk. Not wanting to bother her, she turned to leave. Suddenly Anne looked up. For a moment, Anne, who had always greeted Miep with a smile, looked both alarmed and angry.

Edith came into the room and stood behind Miep. Knowing that Anne did not like being disturbed, Edith said, "Yes, Miep, as you know, we have a daughter who writes."

Anne's diary had taken on a life of its own. Miep said later she had interrupted "an intimate moment in a very, very private friendship." The episode left her uneasy.

Before Anne went into hiding, she spent time with her friends

> *"I want to bring out all kinds of things that lie buried deep in my heart."*
>
> Anne Frank

Anne's writing showed a range of emotions. She was at times serious, funny, angry, or thoughtful.

Dit is een foto, zoals ik me zou wensen, altijd zo te zijn. Dan had ik nog wel een kans om naar Holywood te komen. Maar tegenwoordig zie ik er jammer genoeg meestal anders uit.

Annefrank.

10 Oct. 1942
Vrijdag.

talking, laughing, having fun. She often seemed frivolous and lighthearted. But now that she was living in the annex, isolated from her friends, she had grown more serious. Her writing took on a greater significance.

Anne had a keen eye and ear, and could describe in great detail whatever she saw and heard. Her father said she had a "capacity of observing which was astonishing." She was determined to do well in her schoolwork so she could become a journalist or writer. She even thought of trying to publish one of her stories in a magazine using a made-up name.

While living in the annex, Anne was sometimes prone to sadness, but when she started to write her mood changed. Her writing filled her with pleasure and a sense of accomplishment. On April 5, 1944, she wrote these words in her diary: "When I write I can shake off all my cares. My sorrow disappears, my spirits are revived!"

chapter 9

Cramped Quarters

Anne longed to go outside, to enjoy nature and the sunshine. She wanted to laugh so hard she couldn't stop. But confined to the annex, living in cramped quarters, she could do none of this. Instead she often felt tense and angry, and sometimes lonely and scared. She wanted to share more of her feelings with Margot and her parents, but she felt too often "closed up tighter than a drum."

After spending a year and a half in the annex, Anne wrote, "I long to ride a bike, dance, whistle, look at the world, feel young and know that I'm free, and yet I can't let it show."

Anne, like the other residents of the secret annex, knew she should not complain. Only writing in her diary could ease her frustration. "The nicest part is being able to write down all my thoughts and feelings; otherwise, I'd absolutely suffocate," she wrote.

She often considered the role of women in society. She recognized that in many countries education had opened women's eyes, making it possible for them to obtain equal

Margot was a good student and did well in all subjects. She had a gentle nature, but Anne found it hard to confide in her.

rights, and yet women still did not receive the respect they deserved. This made Anne all the more determined to find a sense of purpose in her own life. She longed to have children one day—she had always loved taking care of babies. But she wanted to do something else as well and not be bound to the house the way her mother had been. Yet it seemed so difficult to find anyone who shared her beliefs.

There were days when Anne felt close to Margot and others when she simply felt annoyed with her. Margot had always been the better student, and it was difficult not to feel jealous. Though Anne wanted so much to please, her parents seemed to take Margot's side. But it wasn't just her parents who favored Margot. Anne thought just about everyone considered Margot not only more intelligent, but also prettier and nicer.

From the time Anne was a little girl, she had had a special relationship with her

Anne's stormy nature made it difficult for her to get along with her family and others, but she tried to make sense of her emotions and to improve her behavior.

father. She always looked forward to his bedtime stories and the poems he would write for her on her birthday. She also treasured a letter he had written her when she was ten years old. "You know how often we share some secret or other," he said. "So often something happens that you and I must talk over. That is not as simple as talking with your big sister—even though, generally speaking, your good humor, your loving personality make it possible for you to slide lightly over things, in your playful manner." Otto explained that he, too, as a child, sometimes acted thoughtlessly and made mistakes. He warned her that she should try to control herself and to swallow the word *but*.

"The main thing," he added, "is to think a little and try to find the right road back. You are not headstrong, and that's why your smile soon returns, if only after a few tears." He ended with these words, "May this joyful laughter, with which you are making your own and other people's lives more beautiful, remain with you." He signed the letter, "Your Pim," using the name Anne had called him since she was a little girl.

No matter how hard Anne tried to be good, her temper

Otto tried to help Anne curb her temper. When she started to lose control, he would whisper "H.J.I.," short for "Hold back" in Dutch.

"The main thing is to think a little and try to find the right road back."

Otto Frank

often got the best of her. She blamed her mother for both big and little problems. She wished her mother would act more like a "real mother"—one in whom Anne could confide all her secrets without the fear of being scolded. At times it felt as if the world was against her and that everyone, but most of all her mother, did nothing but find fault with her. She wrote that her mother's accusations pierced her "like arrows from a tightly strung bow, which are nearly impossible to pull from my body." Anne pretended that the criticisms didn't matter, but they did. "I wish I could ask God to give me another personality, one that doesn't antagonize everyone," she wrote.

One night in April 1943, after nine months in hiding, Anne lay in bed, expecting her father to come say good night and listen to her prayers as usual. Instead, Edith entered the room and asked to hear her prayers. "No, Momsy," she answered.

The words wounded Edith and made her cry. "I can't make you love me," she said to her daughter. Anne knew she was not being kind, but she could not apologize. She was too angry with her mother—and with the world.

As the months passed, Anne became less gloomy, and her attitude toward her mother changed. On January 2, 1944, she reread her pages of her diary entries and could not believe some of the words she'd written. She explained, "I was suffering then (and still do) from moods that kept my head under water (figuratively speaking) and allowed me to see things only from my own perspective." For the first time she saw that she had also been at fault.

Anne told herself she was taking her mother's criticisms too seriously. Had she not been a prisoner to the annex, her feelings would have been less strong. "Those violent outbursts on paper are simply expressions of anger that, in normal life, I could have worked off by locking myself in my room and stamping my foot a few times or calling Mother names behind her back."

Many times Anne thought of the family and friends she had left behind. She missed her grandmothers very much, and when she was asleep at night both of them appeared to her at different times in dreams. Edith's mother was like a guardian angel who watched over and protected her. Her other grandmother seemed so real that Anne could practically feel her "skin of soft crinkly velvet."

Hanneli Goslar, Anne's friend, also came to her in dreams. Anne was sure Hanneli had been captured by the Nazis. Thinking about Hanneli's fate made her want to scream in terror. Her friend's enormous eyes haunted Anne. Why had Anne been spared and not Hanneli?

Anne longed to go back to school, to see her friends, to reclaim the life she'd lost. But instead she had to stay indoors, sharing a small living space with seven others. She could never get away, be on her own, or see new people. Anne confided her deepest secrets and her innermost feelings in her diary. Writing helped her sort through her fears, her sadness, and her anger, and it allowed her to reflect. More often than not, it gave her hope. Anne was the first to admit her writing could raise her "somewhat from 'the depths of despair.'"

Anne's good friend Hanneli appeared to her in a dream. Anne was tormented by the thought that the Nazis would kill her friend.

10

Peter

Cooped up in the annex, Anne was quick to find fault with the other residents. Little things they did annoyed her.

Dr. Pfeffer's tossing and turning made it hard for her to fall asleep at night. He snuck food and ate behind the other residents' backs. He didn't obey the rules of the house. Mrs. van Pels quarreled with Edith and with Mr. van Pels. When Mr. van Pels wanted to sell her fur coat so they would have more money for food, she threw a fit. She screamed, she swore, and she stamped her feet. Mr. van Pels was grouchy, and Edith's nerves were on edge. It wasn't just the people.

Anne was also tired of the food—too many brown beans and navy beans.

Like many girls her age, Anne felt moody and vulnerable. Sometimes she felt on top of the world— smart, witty, pretty. At other times she

At first Peter showed little interest in Anne. But in February 1944 his feelings for her began to change.

felt alone in a world where no one understood her. But unlike many other girls, Anne, living in cramped quarters, had no privacy and no escape. She could never wander outside in the sunshine, or run away from fights and tense emotions. Instead she was always shut up inside the few rooms that had become her home. Anne's emotions overwhelmed her, and she was often depressed.

At first it had seemed that life in the annex was going to be a challenging adventure and an opportunity to spend more time with her father, whose attention she craved. But Anne soon realized the many difficulties of living in such a small space, losing touch with her friends, and facing the uncertainty of the future. The appeal of the daily routine was gone, and Anne's attitude soured. She jumped at every noise and sometimes cried herself to sleep. It took a long time, more than 18 months, for Anne's spirits to revive. Then, in February 1944, she wrote, "A lot has changed for me."

Anne had begun to notice that Peter was taking a special interest in her. It seemed he always had his eyes on her. Whenever they found themselves alone with each other, Peter wanted to talk. He began to confide in her. When he told her how upset he'd become after an argument with Dr. Pfeffer, Anne understood perfectly. She knew exactly how Peter felt, and she was both surprised and pleased that he was being so open with her.

Peter hadn't always been this way. When the van Pels first moved into the annex, Anne decided Peter was too sensitive and lazy. After he complained about various ailments (a blue tongue, a stiff neck), she determined he was also a hypochondriac, always convinced he was sick. But, even during the first months in hiding, she'd admitted to herself that sometimes they could have fun together. They both liked a good laugh, and they enjoyed dressing up to amuse the others.

But now Anne longed for someone she could really talk to. She was beginning to think Peter was just that person. She liked looking into his dark blue eyes.

They began to spend more time together. Anne would go upstairs to Peter's room, and sometimes they would climb up to the attic and look out the window. She liked looking out at the sky and feeling the sunshine on her face. She started to talk to Peter about serious subjects—the war, their future, and what it meant to be Jewish. She trusted him and could say what was in her heart.

Anne wanted to help Peter feel more sure of himself and encouraged him to express his feelings. She knew they both felt things deeply, but they reacted differently when hurt. Anne acted out by splashing water or banging the pots and pans, while Peter kept to himself and said he didn't need friends. Anne was determined to prove him wrong. It would please her no end if he would simply admit he needed her.

"Love, what is love?"

Anne Frank

"Love, what is love?" Anne asked herself. "Love is understanding someone, caring for him, sharing his joys and sorrows." She wished to tell Peter how she felt, but she didn't dare. She longed to see him "morning, noon, and night." Gone was the deep loneliness she had felt earlier. But if ever Anne thought Peter wasn't paying attention to her or that she'd done something to upset him, she became depressed.

The attic was the one quiet place where Anne and Peter could talk alone, away from the adults. They liked to sit on a wooden crate and look out the window, their arms around each other's shoulders.

Then suddenly she would catch Peter looking at her, and she could smile again.

When Anne went up to the attic in the afternoon to fetch the potatoes for dinner, she was often gone longer than necessary. She stopped to chat with Peter on the way. It seemed the more they were together, the more they had to say to each other. They discussed anything and everything—the quarrels in the annex, their parents, Anne's diary, and how much they had both changed since 1942, when they first went into hiding.

The grown-ups liked to gather together at night to hear the news on the radio. They listened to Winston Churchill, the British prime minister, and talked of air raids and the Allies' invasion. They wondered when the war would end. Otto thought the liberation would come soon; Edith wasn't so sure. Mrs. van Pels trembled every time she heard a plane fly overhead.

Anne and Peter sometimes joined the others while they listened to the radio, but they preferred to be by themselves whenever they had the chance. Anne had never been so happy as she was now that she and Peter had become close. "Whenever he looks at me with those eyes, with that smile and that wink, it's as if a light goes on inside me," she wrote.

Anne worried that her sister was feeling left out, but Margot told Anne not to feel sorry for her. She wrote Anne a letter to reassure her and explained that she did feel a little jealous, but that she was also happy for Anne. Margot

From the attic window, Anne and Peter could see the rooftops of Amsterdam and the neighboring Westertoren bell tower.

liked Peter but could never have felt the way Anne did about him. Peter was more like a brother to her. Anne could not stop thinking about Peter and responded to Margot's letter by trying to explain her special closeness to Peter: "In the twilight beside an open window you can say more to each other than in brilliant sunshine."

Anne's parents didn't want Anne to spend so much time with Peter. They worried that Anne and Peter were becoming too attached to each other, and that one of them would be hurt. Mrs. van Pels disapproved and was jealous of all the attention Anne was receiving. Edith told Anne she should stop going to Peter's room. But Anne was not prepared to give him up.

Anne and Peter still sat together in the attic window. They could hear the air-raid sirens, but they were not scared. They felt a closeness neither one had ever known before.

On April 15, 1944, Peter kissed Anne for the first time. It was 9:30 in the evening, and Peter was getting ready to make his nightly rounds to check that the building was secure. Before he left, he touched her cheek and played with her hair. And then he kissed her. The next morning she wrote in her diary, "Remember yesterday's date."

> *"In the twilight beside an open window you can say more to each other than in brilliant sunshine."*
>
> Anne Frank

chapter 11

"The World's Been Turned Upside Down"

While the Franks and their friends hid in the annex, all around them sirens blared and bombs fell. Night after night Anne awoke to the sound of planes and gunfire. In July 1943, heavy bombing left buildings destroyed all over Amsterdam. Anne reported in her diary that more than 200 people had died. Orphaned children, she wrote, were searching in vain for their parents. When Amsterdam's Schiphol Airport was bombed, Anne spent most of the night in her parents' room. She was so scared, she was not sure she'd live to see the morning.

During the war the Allies bombed industrial areas that had been taken over by the Germans.

The residents had more than bombs to fear. Every day they ran the risk of being discovered.

They knew that Willem van Maaren, the head warehouseman, suspected the annex was a secret hiding place, and they were concerned that he might turn them in. Although all the residents tried very hard not to leave any clues that they had used the office at night, they worried that van Maaren might notice if anything were misplaced. Mr. Kugler said that van Maaren set traps to prove

Outside the Annex

Life in Amsterdam was difficult. Food was scarce. Vandalism and theft were becoming common. Citizens were required to turn in their jewelry and metal items, such as kettles and cooking utensils, so the Nazis could use them to make weapons. Businesses were shut down, and international trade had stopped. With the borders closed, residents could not leave the country.

that someone had entered the office. At night he would place a pencil on the edge of a desk. The next morning he would check to see if it had been knocked off. He spread flour on the floor and later looked for footprints. The residents, always careful, now had to become even more cautious.

One evening, the residents heard a barrel falling in the warehouse and someone fiddling with the door. Otto and Peter went downstairs to see what was happening. They came back up to report they had heard doors banging. Burglars must have forced their way into the warehouse and then been scared off by Otto's and Peter's footsteps. All night the Franks worried that the police would find the doors unlocked, come inside to investigate, and discover the hiding place.

A few months later the intruders struck again. Early that morning, Peter went down to the warehouse before the employees arrived and discovered that the door to the street was open. Fearing a burglary, he went back upstairs. The residents made as little noise as possible; they dressed silently, and they didn't wash or let the water run. Finally, Mr. Kugler came upstairs and

The residents of the Secret Annex dreaded the sound of creaking stairs that might signal the presence of an intruder.

confirmed their suspicions. Burglars had used a crowbar to force the door open. Missing were two cashboxes, containing money and ration coupons for 330 pounds of sugar—enough sugar to last all of them a year.

Yet another night, Mr. van Pels went downstairs after dinner and discovered that someone had entered the office, leaving it in chaos. The next morning, Peter found the front door open. Mr. Kugler's new briefcase was missing. The residents started to worry that a burglar had been hiding in the office while Mr. van Pels was downstairs. Could he have heard Mr. van Pels on the steps and then hidden in a closet? Was it possible he had also seen Mr. van Pels?

The most frightening incident came in April of 1944. One evening, Peter heard a disturbing noise—two loud bangs that echoed through the annex. He went downstairs to find a large panel missing from the door to the street. He ran upstairs to tell the others and then brought Otto, Mr. van Pels, and Dr. Pfeffer down to investigate. There in the warehouse they saw the burglars. Mr. van Pels yelled, "Police!" and the burglars fled. The residents were replacing the panel on the door when a man and woman passed by and shone a flashlight inside the warehouse. Otto and the others quickly turned away, but they worried that the couple had seen them.

Later that night, all the residents sat waiting, tense and silent. At 11:00 PM they heard footsteps on the stairs. Then the moving bookcase rattled. A can fell. Anne was sure that any minute the Gestapo were going to break down the bookcase. Then there was quiet. Had the Gestapo left, or were they standing guard outside?

The eight residents lay down in the darkness on the top floor and tried to sleep. They took turns going to the bathroom in a metal wastepaper basket. Of all of them, Mrs. van Pels was the most frightened. Anne tried to reassure her.

The next day the office was closed for a holiday, and none of the helpers or other employees planned to come to work. Otto crept down to the office, phoned Mr. Kleiman, told him what had happened, and asked that Miep's husband Jan come investigate. Anne and the other residents spent the morning in suspense. Finally they heard a knocking on the

bookcase. This could signal one of two possibilities: Jan's arrival—or the return of the police and their impending arrest. Mrs. van Pels looked as if she was about to faint.

> *"We've been strongly reminded of the fact that we're Jews in chains."*
>
> Anne Frank

When both Jan and Miep entered, the residents cried with relief. Jan nailed a board over the hole in the door. Then they all decided Jan and Miep should tell the police about the incident. If they did not report the attempted burglary and the police were to learn about it on their own, it would seem suspicious that no one had filed a report.

Over the next few days Jan uncovered part of the mystery surrounding the break-in. The night watchman, Mr. Sleegers, who knew nothing of the residents in hiding, told Jan that he had discovered the hole in the door, reported it to a policeman, and together the two men had searched the building. This explained the rattling of the bookcase. Then Mr. van Hoeven, a grocer who made deliveries to the office, told Jan that he and his wife had been walking by the office one night and saw a hole in the door. They had used their flashlight to investigate but had decided not to report the vandalism to the police. He admitted to Jan that he suspected there were Jews hiding inside and he did not want to put them at greater risk.

This time the residents were spared, but they could not escape the great danger all around them.

"We've been strongly reminded of the fact that we're Jews in chains," Anne wrote, "chained to one spot, without any rights." Anne had thought she was going to die that night. She was stunned the police had not found them. None of them had ever been in such great danger. But the incident, as frightening as it was, gave Anne strength. If she survived the war, she could try to accomplish her dreams—to make her voice heard and the world a better place.

Anne wondered why millions could be spent on war, but nothing on medical scientists, artists, and the poor. She asked herself why some people had no food and others let food go to waste. Across Holland—and also in the annex—food was becoming scarce.

"Every day I feel myself maturing, I feel liberation drawing near."

Anne Frank

Anne wrote that through the ages Jews had been made to suffer, but that God would lift them up again.

They still had beans and potatoes to eat, and occasionally turnip greens, rotten carrots, or beet salad. Once a week they enjoyed a slice of liverwurst.

Anne marveled that they could get by on so little. She tried to help by cleaning the dining table, but the dishcloth they had purchased before they went into hiding was now in shreds. Otto's trousers were torn and his shaving brush was worn thin. Edith and Margot shared the same three undershirts all winter long.

Anne tried to keep her handwriting very neat, even when her words conveyed passionate emotions.

They all had to find ways to pass the time without making too much noise. When Edith wasn't reading, she was knitting. Peter often climbed up to the attic, where he kept his tools, but hammering was out of the question during the day. Dr. Pfeffer provided dental care for all the residents, cleaning their teeth on a regular basis.

The helpers did what they could to celebrate special occasions and even introduced the residents to some Christian holidays. On December 5, St. Nicholas Eve, when Dutch children honor their patron saint and look forward to receiving presents, Miep and Bep decorated a basket, filled it with little presents they had made, and wrote funny rhyming poems for each of the residents. And on Christmas, Miep brought them more presents and baked a cake for the occasion—with the words "Peace 1944" written on top. All the residents were touched, but Anne was the most excited.

The helpers also tried to quiet the residents' fears and did not often share the most devastating news of the war. Anne was amazed that the helpers never complained of the risks they were taking. On January 28, 1944, she wrote in her diary, "While others display their heroism in battle or against the Germans, our helpers prove theirs every day by their good spirits and affection."

Gerrit Bolkestein, the Dutch minister of Education, lived in London during the war. An announcement he made on the BBC inspired Anne to rewrite her diary so that it could be published after the war.

In school, Anne had been amusing and flirtatious, quick to make a joke. Her life changed drastically once she went into hiding. At first she'd had a hard time adjusting and could only cope by talking back to her parents and sister. Then she became overcome with loneliness. But, by the summer of 1943, after a year in hiding, she started to feel less sad and more resilient. The little things people said didn't bother her as much. She felt the others considered her more of a grown-up and less of a child. Even Margot was treating her more like a real friend than a younger sister.

After more than a year and a half of confinement, Anne had become less frightened. On January 30, 1944, she stood at the top of the stairs and heard the German planes fly back and forth. "I looked up at the sky and trusted in God," she wrote. She saw more beauty in nature, and her faith in God grew. She felt a new contentment, and she wanted to share this feeling with Peter.

Anne started writing in this diary, a gift from her parents, on June 12, 1942. She continued writing in it until she filled the last page on December 5, 1942.

As Anne worked on her diary and gained more confidence in her writing, she felt fulfilled in a way she'd never known. In March of 1944, Anne heard a radio broadcast from Gerrit Bolkestein, a government official living in exile in London. He talked about the importance of keeping a record of the war, and said that a collection of diaries and letters written during wartime would be published after the war ended. Anne had been writing in her diary for almost two years. Surely the end of the war would come soon, just as everyone predicted. Anne decided to prepare her diary for publication. She started to recopy it and, in the process, made revisions—cutting a few sentences and adding others. She wanted to call her book *The Secret Annex* so that it would appeal to readers who would think it was a detective story.

June 6, 1944: D Day

On June 6, 1944, 156,000 British, Canadian, and American troops landed on the shores of Normandy in France. The Allies, under the command of General Dwight D. Eisenhower, had carefully planned the invasion, designed to take them into German-occupied Europe and lead to victory over the Nazis.

Everyone in the annex tried to predict the starting date of the British invasion that would bring victory to the Allies. Otto, the most optimistic, cast his bet that it would begin soon. But by May 20, 1944, there was still no sign of the promised invasion. Otto lost his bet and had to give Mrs. van Pels five jars of yogurt. Nothing seemed certain. Anne wrote, "The world's been turned upside down.…Unless you're a Nazi, you don't know what's going to happen to you from one day to the next."

Then, on June 6, 1944, the BBC radio announced, "This is D Day," signaling the beginning of the Allied invasion of Europe. That night, Anne recorded the "huge commotion in the Annex" and asked, "Is this really the beginning of the long-awaited liberation?"

News of the invasion filled Anne with hope. She listened to reports of the war on the radio, noting in her diary the progress the Allies made. At the same time, she was turning

inward, thinking about her own faults. She was determined to become a better person. She explained, "I also know that I want to change,

> ## "We can start now, start slowly changing the world."
>
> Anne Frank

will change, and already have changed greatly!"

Anne, extremely self-aware, believed she could shape her own character. She had great courage and could face any difficulty. But she knew she had many imperfections, and she struggled to improve. No one, not even her father who knew her best, could understand how hard she tried and how much she wanted to find a sense of purpose in her own life.

It was easy to talk to Peter. They discussed so many things, and yet had she ever revealed to him the deepest secrets of her heart? In some ways he disappointed her. He seemed young, and he had too little willpower. But she still longed to be with him, and her mixed feelings confused her.

On August 1, 1944, Anne wrote that she felt split in two. One side of her was exuberant and cheerful, always ready for a laugh. Her other side was loving and gentle. People who knew her only saw the lighthearted Anne, but she hid the other Anne, the more thoughtful Anne. She wanted to bring together her two sides and "keep trying to find a way to become what I'd like to be."

Anne never again wrote in her diary.

12

"The Gestapo Is Here"

On the morning of August 4, 1944, Gestapo officer Karl Silberbauer and several Dutch Nazi policemen entered the front office at 263 Prinsengracht. Silberbauer pointed a gun at Mr. Kleiman, Miep, and Bep and told them to sit quietly. Mr. Kleiman and Miep were terrified, but tried to appear calm. Bep couldn't help shaking.

Mr. Kugler heard the commotion and opened his office door. Silberbauer, pistol in hand, asked him who was in charge. Mr. Kugler responded that he was. Silberbauer informed Mr. Kugler that he was looking for secret weapons and demanded to see each room. Mr. Kugler wanted to appear cooperative, opening cabinet doors and boxes in the rooms on the second floor. Then Silberbauer insisted on going to the third floor.

Did they already know about the secret hiding place? Mr. Kugler wasn't sure. The Gestapo examined the storerooms and

The Gestapo investigated tips informing them about the location of Jews in hiding.

then stepped onto the landing near the bookcase. Mr. Kugler watched in horror as they started taking the books and boxes off the bookcase. They tried several times to move the bookcase but could not. Then they shook it forcefully. The hook came unfastened, and it moved.

With their guns drawn, the police told Mr. Kugler to lead the way. They entered the Franks' bedroom. Mr. Kugler saw Edith first. He spoke softly, "The Gestapo is here."

One of the policemen looked in Anne's room and found Anne and Margot. The girls were in shock. They had dreaded this moment for so many months, but there was nothing that could have prepared them for it.

The other policemen climbed the steep staircase. Otto was in Peter's room helping Peter with his English lesson. Dr. Pfeffer was with Mr. and Mrs. van Pels in their room. Silberbauer ordered them to join the others downstairs.

The eight residents stood together silently in the Franks' bedroom. They did not move, but kept their hands held high, as the police had instructed. Margot started to cry. Silberbauer demanded to know where they kept their money, jewelry, and any other valuables. Otto pointed to a cupboard. Silberbauer picked up the briefcase that Anne had used for storing her diary and papers. He shook out the contents. The notebooks and loose papers fell to the floor. Silberbauer put the Franks' cash box and their menorah into the briefcase.

Then Silberbauer noticed an army footlocker trunk. "Where did you get this?" he demanded. Otto answered that he had been a German officer during World War I. Silberbauer looked surprised. He asked Otto why he had taken the risk of going into hiding. If only he had registered as a Jew, Silberbauer said, as a German officer he would have been given special privileges and sent to Theresienstadt, a camp in Czechoslovakia, where Jews were treated better than they were at other concentration camps. But Otto had been given no assurance that he and his family would have been sent there—or that they would have remained safe.

Now that Silberbauer knew Otto had been a German army officer, he showed more respect toward the prisoners. He gave them time to gather their belongings while he went to the office to call for transportation.

Silberbauer also arrested Mr. Kugler and Mr. Kleiman. Bep had left the building while the police were upstairs, but Silberbauer did not notice that she was missing. He turned to Miep. "Now, it's your turn," he said.

Miep recognized his accent.

The Puls moving company in Amsterdam was employed by the Nazis to empty Jewish residences and send the goods to Germany.

It was Viennese—like hers. She told him she was born in Vienna and asked him if he also was. Miep showed him her identity card stating she had been born in Vienna and married a Dutchman. Silberbauer began to shout and curse, asking, "Aren't you ashamed to be helping Jews?"

He stopped yelling and looked at her in silence. Then he told her she could stay—but if she ever tried to run away, he would arrest her husband. Miep insisted that her husband had not been involved. Silberbauer laughed and told her he would return to check on her.

The Gestapo ordered the residents of the Secret Annex, Mr. Kugler, and Mr. Kleiman to leave the building and climb into the police truck. Anne followed the others downstairs. For the first time in more than two years, she stepped outside into fresh air. She could see the sparkling water in the canal and feel the warm sun on her face. But she could not taste the freedom she had hoped would be hers. She was no longer a prisoner of the annex—now she was a prisoner of the Nazis.

Confiscated Valuables

After Jews were arrested, the Nazis took possession of their household items. They shipped them to Germany and distributed them to Nazi officials. When the Nazi moving truck arrived at 263 Prinsengracht, Miep, who had already collected most of Anne's papers, asked van Maaren, a warehouse employee, to go with the movers into the annex, pretend to tidy up, and retrieve any remaining papers. Miep took the papers for safekeeping—the movers took everything else.

chapter 13

Westerbork

N azi officer Karl Silberbauer brought the ten people he had arrested to Gestapo headquarters. He warned Mr. Kugler and Mr. Kleiman, "Caught with them, you will be hanged with them." But the two helpers' lives were spared. Silberbauer detained the two men in prison, and five weeks later sent them to a transit camp in nearby Amersfoort. Both men were made to suffer, and Mr. Kugler was beaten with a club, yet they were treated better than the Jewish prisoners.

The Gestapo questioned the Franks, the van Pelses, and Dr. Pfeffer to try to gain information about other Jews, but they learned nothing. The prisoners spent several days in jail. Then the Nazis took them to Central Station to board a train for Westerbork, a transit camp 80 miles northeast of Amsterdam.

At Central Station in Amsterdam, prisoners board a train for Westerbork. More than 100,000 Dutch Jews were sent to Westerbork between 1942 and 1944.

Jews were allowed to take suitcases with them to Westerbork. But once they arrived, they were forced to turn over their belongings.

Here inmates were forced to work, but did not face the harsh conditions at other camps in Germany or Poland. There were no killing centers at Westerbork.

Although Anne was a captive, the train journey came as a welcome change after more than two years in the annex. Otto remembered how much Anne enjoyed sitting by the window: "It was summer outside. Meadows, stubble fields and villages flew by....It was like freedom for her."

The camp at Westerbork was surrounded by barbed wire. Inside were more than 100 barracks with wooden bunks. The residents of the Secret Annex were sent to the S barracks—the punishment barracks for criminals, including Jews who had gone into hiding. The Nazis took away the prisoners' clothes and shoes and gave them blue overalls with a red bib and wooden clogs to wear.

Both the men's and women's barracks were crowded, dirty, and flea-ridden. As many as 300 prisoners were housed in one barracks. They had water to wash themselves, but no soap. Edith felt anxious about Anne and Margot and tried to keep them by her side. She spoke very little.

All the prisoners had to participate in roll calls—standing in rows of five for more than an hour. Starting at 5:00AM, Edith, Margot, Anne, and Mrs. van Pels began their work: They sat at long tables and cut open used batteries. They threw tar in one basket, carbon bars in a second, and metal caps in a third. Opening the batteries produced great quantities of brown dust that made it difficult to breathe.

Many of the prisoners at Westerbork were frustrated and miserable. But Anne remained cheerful. She spent time with Peter and other people her own age. She enjoyed being outdoors again and looked forward to the ballgames and exercise sessions in the afternoon. And after eating so many potatoes in the annex, the food at Westerbork—oatmeal for breakfast, chicken for dinner—came as a welcome change.

But Anne was not there long before she became ill and was sent to the infirmary. Otto was allowed to visit her in the evenings. He spent hours by her bed, telling her stories just the way he had done when she

Men and women slept in separate barracks at Westerbork. Anne, Edith, and Margot were put into a crowded room with 300 other women.

was little. The stories helped Anne recover. Later, a 12-year-old boy who was housed in the women's barracks with his mother also became ill. Anne treated him as Otto had treated her. They spent the long evenings together talking about religion and God.

In August 1944, the Germans were beginning to lose the war, and the number of transports to death camps decreased. Many hoped that they had come to an end.

But they were sadly mistaken. The Franks only remained at Westerbork for three weeks. On the evening of September 2, 1944, a Nazi officer read out each of their names. The next morning

Transit Camps

The Nazis sent the Jews to transit camps before moving them to concentration camps. Conditions at transit camps were not as harsh, nor as difficult, as they were at other camps. At Westerbork and other transit camps, inmates were forced to work until they were transferred. They had to work in the kitchen, clean the barracks, or perform menial tasks such as breaking up batteries. One hundred thousand Jews were deported from Westerbork, most to extermination (death) camps at Auschwitz and Sobibor.

they would be put on a transport and sent away.

The Franks, the van Pelses, and Dr. Pfeffer were among the 498 men, 442 women, and 79 children to be called. Theirs was the last train to take Jews from Westerbork to Auschwitz, the largest killing center in Nazi-controlled territory.

14

Auschwitz

The Franks, the van Pelses, and Dr. Pfeffer rode in a closed car on a freight train for three days and three nights. With so many people crowded into the car, there was no room to lie down. Some stood while others sat on the straw lining the floor. They had almost no food, only a little bread and beet marmalade provided by the SS, the Nazi guards who oversaw the concentration camps. The prisoners took turns peering through the one small, barred window in the car. Anne watched

A sign over the entrance to Auschwitz read ARBEIT MACHT FREI, meaning "Work makes one free." No prisoner became free, however, until the camp was liberated in 1945.

the rain fall as they crossed into Germany, on their way to Auschwitz, a concentration camp in Poland. The Franks, like the others in the car, did not talk much, but they did discuss a meeting place in case they became separated: Otto's mother's home in Switzerland.

SS guards stood at attention as the train pulled into Auschwitz in the dark of night. Large, fierce dogs, ready to pounce, waited by their side. "Women to the left! Men to the right!" came a voice from the loudspeaker.

For the first time since they had gone into hiding, Edith, Anne, and Margot would not get to see Otto. Even at Westerbork, where men and women were assigned to sleep in separate barracks, the Franks had seen one another every day. But now the women were made to march for an hour to the women's camp. Trucks were provided for small children, the sick, and those too weak to walk. They were never seen again. Of the 1,019 passengers on the Franks' transport, 549 were immediately taken to the gas chambers.

Lenie de Jong, who had met the Franks at Westerbork and Auschwitz, said later, "Auschwitz was really the end of everything; the clay soil always with standing water; a huge quagmire without a sprig of green. No fly flew there. Not a bird, of course, nothing. There was nothing, nothing that looked alive, no flower, nothing, absolutely nothing." An electrically charged barbed wire fence surrounded the camp. No escape was possible.

As soon as the inmates arrived, the Nazis set out to humiliate them and take away

Each wooden bunk was meant for two people to lie on lengthwise, but barracks were often so crowded that five or six people had to lie across a bunk.

their personal identities. They wanted to make their prisoners look and dress alike and referred to them not by name, but by number. The prisoners' heads were shaved, and numbers were tattooed on their left forearms. Men were made to wear striped jackets and pants, and women gray dresses, cut like sacks. They were treated cruelly and given very little to eat and only dirty water to drink.

At night, Edith and the two girls were crammed together with more than one thousand people in Women's Block 29. The barracks had neither ventilation nor heat—only a strong odor. There were no bathrooms and certainly no privacy. The women were taken to a toilet three times a day and otherwise had to use a bucket. Once a week the guards brought them to a

large shower stall where they could wash, but they had only a little water and no soap. Then the guards sprayed them with disinfectant powder to rid them of lice.

Every morning and every evening all the prisoners were forced to participate in the dreaded roll call. They stood in rows, often for more than two hours. It was difficult to stand still with their arms held high. Sometimes they were clothed; at other times they stood naked in the rain or cold.

After the morning roll call, the guards distributed

Auschwitz

Between 1940 and 1945, more than one million people were killed at Auschwitz-Birkenau, the largest Nazi death camp. Up to two thousand people at a time were locked into a gas chamber and poisoned. Dr. Josef Mengele, an SS doctor, decided which prisoners would be selected for the gas chamber. Others were used in medical experiments. Some prisoners chose to commit suicide by walking into the electrically charged barbed wire fence that surrounded the camp.

one piece of bread and one cup of coffee to every five people. Then the prisoners started their work. Anne, Margot, and Edith were assigned to digging up squares of grass and placing them in piles. Wherever they went, they always stayed close to one another. They were never far from the black smoke that rose from the crematorium, the building where the bodies were burned. Anne knew that any one of them could be the next victim.

Anne was often sad, but she remained sweet and caring. She was in charge of distributing the bread in the barracks and did it as fairly as she could. Many times she went out of her way to help others, never giving up hope. When her mother's friend Rosa de Winter became ill, Anne did what most would have thought impossible. She managed to obtain an extra cup of coffee she could give to Rosa—an act of kindness Rosa would never forget.

It was hard for Anne to witness what was happening at Auschwitz. She cried when she saw a group of young girls, all naked, being marched to the gas chambers. Other prisoners no longer reacted. They had shut themselves off from the suffering that surrounded them. Rosa, who survived Auschwitz, tried to explain, "You cannot imagine how soon most of us came to the end of our tears." She recognized that Anne was different: Anne never stopped feeling.

On October 27, 1944, the SS chose the youngest and healthiest prisoners to be sent to Czechoslovakia to work in a weapons factory. Edith and Margot were selected, but not Anne. The guards passed over her because she had developed scabies, a skin disease that caused raw sores and painful itching. Edith insisted she would not leave without both her daughters. She was so persuasive that the SS allowed both Edith and Margot to remain behind with Anne.

Three days later the Nazis prepared for another selection. Knowing that the Russian army would soon reach Auschwitz and take control, the Germans wanted to empty the camp before the Allies could take control. They planned to take those who were healthiest to camps in Germany. The others they would leave behind to die in the gas chambers. The Nazis ordered the women to strip and examined them under a searchlight. Edith was put with the old and sick, those condemned to the gas chambers. But Margot and Anne were among the group chosen for deportation to Bergen-Belsen, a German concentration camp.

Edith and Rosa de Winter were together as they were led to the gas chambers. But in the dark of night, Edith, Rosa, and several other women slipped away from the SS guards and joined another group of prisoners. The SS, usually mindful and alert, never noticed.

Later Edith became ill and was put in the infirmary. She was so weak she could not eat. She hid the bread that was given to her under the blanket. When Rosa visited her, Edith told her she was saving it for her husband and children.

Edith died at Auschwitz on January 6, 1945.

Guards kept watch over the movements of all the prisoners at Auschwitz, making it impossible for them to escape.

chapter **15**

Across the Barbed Wire Fence

For the second time, Anne and Margot made a journey in a crowded cattle car. They rode for five days and nights, making frequent stops in areas where there was heavy bombing. They had little to wear, and the air was bitter cold. The SS provided bread, a slice of cheese, and water for the journey. Anne and Margot huddled together while, all around them, people wept.

At Bergen-Belsen there were not enough barracks to house the new inmates. Anne and Margot and the group from Auschwitz were put in tents. One night, in a violent thunderstorm, the tent where they were sleeping collapsed, and many people were seriously injured. Anne and Margot spent several nights sleeping under the fallen tent, and were then crowded into the wooden and stone barracks shared by the other inmates.

The War Continues

1944 and early 1945 saw Allied victories on a number of fronts. Parts of Holland were liberated. The Russians advanced through northern Europe. In France and Belgium, the Allies won the Battle of the Bulge. But areas in Holland still under Nazi control faced the "Hunger Winter"; food was scarce, and homes were without heat or power. Resisters were arrested and killed. All of Holland would not be freed until May 1945.

A large group of Dutch children were housed at Bergen-Belsen. Because they were *mischlinge* (children from mixed marriages), they had been spared the gas chamber. Anne and Margot visited them often and took comfort in telling them stories. But the two sisters had only to look around them to be reminded once again of death. The conditions at the camp had become so unsanitary and disease so widespread that prisoners were dying by the thousands.

With roads blocked and train tracks damaged, the Germans were able to procure very little food for the prisoners. Only small amounts were available, sometimes stale bread, and occasionally onions and boiled cabbage. Margot, weakened from malnutrition, became sick with typhus. The freezing temperatures made her more miserable. Anne tried to keep her spirits up, but Margot's condition only grew worse.

Anne still hoped she might be able to help her sister. In January 1945, she was reunited with her old friend Hanneli Goslar in Bergen-Belsen.

By the end of the war, the only traces left of many prisoners were the shoes they were forced to surrender. At the end of the war, thousands of shoes were found in piles at concentration camps.

Hanneli's mother had died in childbirth in October 1942, only a few months after the Franks had gone into hiding. On May 20, 1943, Hanneli, her father and sister were arrested in a round-up and taken to Westerbork. They remained there until February 1944, when they were deported to Bergen-Belsen.

The Nazis had chosen a group of prominent Jews to be sent to Bergen-Belsen and used as hostages in exchange for German prisoners of war. This group lived in a section at Bergen-Belsen where prisoners received special treatment. Because Hanneli's father was politically important in Amsterdam, the Goslars found themselves among this group.

One of the prisoners in this section, a woman from Amsterdam who knew both the Franks and the Goslars, heard that Anne was also at Bergen-Belsen—at the other camp, on the other side of the high barbed wire fence. She quickly found Hanneli to tell her the news. Hanneli, who until then had thought the Franks were living safely in Switzerland, was bewildered and did not know what to believe.

All day Hanneli waited for dark. She knew a small opening had been made in the fence

High barbed wire fences surrounded the camp.

separating the camps so that prisoners could talk to those on the other side. When evening came, she crept outside to the fence to look

for the opening. Once she found it, she called out in Dutch to see if anyone on the other side knew Anne Frank. Word traveled among the inmates, and then suddenly Hanneli was surprised to hear a familiar voice. Mrs. van Pels was standing on the other side of the fence! She had escaped the gas chambers. Mrs. van Pels told Hanneli she would go look for Anne. So, Hanneli thought, Anne had not gone to Switzerland after all, but was in the Bergen-Belsen death camp.

Hanneli could hardly believe what was happening. She was excited to see her friend but horrified to think that she was in the concentration camp. Anne appeared in a striped uniform, her head shaven, her body shrunken. It was a sad meeting for the two friends. Hanneli told Anne that Mrs. Goslar had died before they were captured, and now Mr. Goslar was very ill. Anne answered, telling Hanneli she feared she had lost both her parents. Her mother had been selected for the gas chamber. She had heard nothing of her father, but very likely he had met the same fate. Now Margot was sick with typhus. The two girls arranged to meet again. Anne asked Hanneli if it would be possible for her to bring a little food so that she could give it to Margot.

Prisoners in Hanneli's camp, unlike Anne, were allowed to receive small amounts of food from the Red Cross. Hanneli worked on putting together a package to give Anne and collected cubes of sugar, some cheese, crackers, and a pair of black cotton stockings. When she met Anne two nights later she threw the package over the fence. It fell on the ground, but another woman quickly grabbed it and ran away with it. Anne started to sob. She had lost the little food that might make all the difference to Margot.

Hanneli told Anne that she would try again another night. Once more Hanneli persuaded other prisoners to give up some of their food. She took the crackers and cheese they offered and tied them up in a sweater. She waited for nightfall and then met Anne at the fence. She threw the package high in the air and over the fence. This time Anne caught it.

That was the last time the two girls saw each other. Mr. Goslar became so ill that Hanneli could not leave his side. She returned later to the fence, but Anne never appeared.

The typhus spread, and before long Anne was suffering from it, too. That winter the disease killed thousands at Bergen-Belsen. Every day Anne and Margot grew weaker and thinner, and their eyes appeared darker and deeper. Then one night, Margot lost consciousness and died, falling from the top bunk to the stone floor of the barracks.

Anne's condition worsened, and she became delirious, losing touch with reality. Desperate to rid herself of lice and fleas, she took off all her clothes. She wrapped herself in a blanket, but she could not stop shivering. Jannie Brilleslijper, a prisoner who worked as a nurse, brought her water, but there was little else she or anyone could do.

Anne died in early March, two or three days after Margot. The exact day is not known. She had suffered from malnutrition and typhus; she was killed by human cruelty.

After the British liberated Bergen-Belsen on April 15, 1945—just weeks after Anne died—the typhus-infected buildings were burned to prevent the spread of infection.

chapter 16

"I Never Stop Thinking of Them"

At Auschwitz, Otto became ill and was put in the infirmary. Peter came every day to visit and bring Otto food. Then, in January 1945, as the Russians advanced toward Auschwitz, the Nazis ordered all those who were healthy and fit to prepare to leave the camp. Peter told Otto he had received orders to leave. Otto worried that Peter would only face more danger if he left Auschwitz. He urged Peter to stay behind and hide in the infirmary.

But Peter did not want to risk getting caught. He was one of the 60,000 prisoners who departed Auschwitz on January 17 in the Nazi evacuation. Led by German soldiers on a long march, they walked across Poland in freezing temperatures on icy roads. When Peter and the others reached Austria, they were put in another concentration camp, this time farther away from the Russian soldiers.

The prisoners who stayed behind, too weak to march, survived on the food the Nazis had abandoned. After 10 days, German SS officers returned with machine guns. They rounded up the prisoners and ordered them to stand in a line. Otto thought he and the other prisoners would be shot. He stood waiting as the SS aimed their guns. They prepared

This map of Europe shows the advance of the Allies into territories occupied by Germany (green arrows), the advance of the Russian troops (red arrows), and the route Otto took from Auschwitz (blue arrows) before he could return home to Amsterdam.

to fire. Then, suddenly, there was a huge explosion. The noise was deafening. The SS turned their heads to see what had caused the commotion. Then they panicked. The Russians were approaching; the Nazis fled without firing.

Otto and the other prisoners were dumbstruck. Only a short moment ago they had faced certain execution, and now the Russians were about to set them free.

When the troops entered Auschwitz, the prisoners cheered and embraced the Russian soldiers. With only limited medical supplies, the Russians cared for the sick as best they could. They shared their food with the prisoners and provided hope that the war would soon come to an end.

Liberation of the Concentration Camps

Russian soldiers freed the 7,650 remaining prisoners at Auschwitz on January 27, 1945. The Russians provided food, but many of the prisoners were too sick to digest it. Of those who were liberated half would die within a few days. Of the 41,000 prisoners held at Bergen-Belsen, 37,000 died of starvation and disease. The British liberated the remaining prisoners on April 15, 1945, within several weeks of Anne's death.

Those who had survived Auschwitz could not return to the Netherlands while it was occupied by the Nazis. Otto, like the others, waited. On March 5, 1945, the Russians brought Otto and the other survivors by train from Auschwitz to Katowice, a city in Poland.

For several weeks, the survivors waited for a train that would take them to Odessa, a Russian port on the Black Sea. From there the Russians planned to send them home by ship. Otto had been close to starvation at Auschwitz, but now he began to recover and his appetite returned.

In Katowice, the survivors were housed in a school building. The men and women, who for so long had been separated in different camps, could now talk to one another and gather information about their families and friends.

Rosa de Winter, Edith's friend from Auschwitz, found Otto sitting at a long table. She told him that she had seen his wife and children in the barracks. She talked about how much time they had spent together and how close and caring they had been. In spite of everything, Anne had tried to keep her spirits up. But Rosa had lost touch with Margot and Anne in late October. The girls were selected for deportation to another camp, Rosa explained. Edith, malnourished and separated from her children, had never recovered. She died from grief and exhaustion. Otto listened—he could not speak. Then he turned away.

The train that would take the survivors to Odessa finally pulled into the station on March 31, 1945. Otto boarded the train for the long journey. Once they reached Odessa, the passengers were made to wait again, this time for a ship that would take them from the Black Sea, across the Mediterranean, all the way to Marseilles, a port in southern France. The Germans had surrendered—now Otto was free to return home.

On May 19, 1945, the *Monoway*, a troop transport ship, set sail with Otto and other survivors on board. Otto dared to hope that upon reaching Amsterdam he would be reunited with his children. Eight days later, the SS *Monoway* docked in Marseilles. A band played and a splendid reception greeted the ship. But Otto was in no mood to celebrate. He thought only of his children and was eager to return home.

Otto arrived in Amsterdam on June 3, 1945. He went first to the home of Miep and Jan Gies. They immediately took him in, feeding him dinner and giving him a bed to sleep in.

Otto asked about Margot and Anne, but Miep and Jan had heard nothing.

Otto continued to live with Miep and Jan and soon went back to work at Opekta, settling into his former office in the building where he had lived in hiding for 25 months. He was relieved to learn that Miep, Jan, and Bep were never arrested and that both Victor Kugler and Johannes Kleiman had returned safely from Dutch concentration camps. But Otto still did not know if Anne and Margot were alive. In a letter to his mother, who had remained in Switzerland throughout the war, Otto wrote, "I never stop thinking about them."

As survivors returned to Amsterdam, Otto questioned everyone about his daughters.

Learning that Anne and Margot

The port of Marseilles in France was damaged by dynamite during the war. Otto arrived here on May 29, 1945, on his long journey home.

had been sent away from Auschwitz to Bergen-Belsen, he hung on to the hope that they had survived. He placed ads in local newspapers requesting information, and he routinely checked the lists of the missing, published by the Dutch Red Cross. An "X" signified that a person had died, but there was no "X" next to Margot and Anne's names.

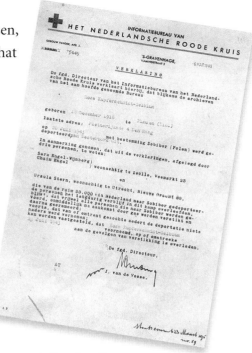

Letters from the Red Cross, such as this one, informed citizens about their missing relatives.

Then in July 1945, Otto received a letter from Jannie Brilleslijper, now a nurse in Rotterdam. He and Miep were both in the front office. Miep watched Otto read the letter. Then Otto turned toward her and said, "Margot and Anne are not coming back." They were both silent. Otto went into his own office and shut the door.

Later Miep opened her desk drawer and pulled out Anne's diaries and loose papers. She had never read them. She carried them into Otto's office and placed them on his desk. "Here is your daughter Anne's legacy to you," she said.

Otto remained in his office and asked not to be disturbed.

Otto could not bring himself to read Anne's diary right away, but after a time, he opened it, and cried as he read Anne's words. He was overcome with a deep sadness. He missed his daughters terribly.

Otto traveled to Rotterdam to visit Jannie Brilleslijper, the nurse who had last seen his daughters alive. He wanted to hear about Anne

Anne's diary showed Otto sides of Anne he had never known.

and Margot's last days at Bergen-Belsen. Jannie shared all that she could remember, knowing how much he missed them. It was difficult to talk, but she told him how their bodies were wrapped in blankets and buried with the many others who had died at Bergen-Belsen.

As the weeks passed, Otto began to absorb what he had read. He realized how much there was about Anne that he had not known before, even though he and his daughter had always enjoyed a close relationship. Through her diary Anne had shown him parts of herself that were unfamiliar to him—the depth of her emotions, her self-criticism, and her desire to improve herself. Then, too, there was her interest in

God and her appreciation of nature—all new to him. He had not known how much a glimpse of the blue sky or the chestnut tree or the seagulls flying in the distance had meant to her. And now he was amazed by all that Anne's diary revealed to him.

There was an exchange of letters between Anne and Margot included in the diary that gave him great pleasure to read. He was happy to see how close the two sisters had become. Much of what Anne said about her relationship with her mother was painful to read, but Otto took comfort in knowing that later, while still confined to the annex, Anne recognized that the frequent disagreements were also her own fault.

Otto translated excerpts of the diary into German and sent them to his mother to read. He then began to type the entire

"Anne's legacy"

Who Betrayed the Franks?

In 1963, Karl Silberbauer, the Nazi officer who arrested the Franks, reported that the Gestapo had learned of the annex from a Dutch drugstore employee. Another suspect was a Dutch Nazi party member who had betrayed Jews, non-Jews, and members of his own family in exchange for money. Yet there is still no concrete evidence. To this day, the identity of the betrayer remains a mystery that historians and biographers seek to unravel.

manuscript. Otto showed the diary to friends, many of whom had also survived the concentration camps. When he asked for their opinion on publishing the diary, a few answered that there would be little interest in the diary. Some objected to certain passages they considered too personal. Anne would want her feelings toward her mother and Peter to remain private. Most, however, urged Otto to publish the diary. They related personally to Anne's experience and recognized both the literary and historical significance of the diary.

On April 3, 1946, a headline in the newspaper, *Het Parool*, "Voice of a Child," caught Otto's eye. Otto read on and discovered that the article, written by Jan Romein, a history professor at the University of Amsterdam, was about Anne. Much to Otto's surprise, Professor Romein had been given a copy of the diary and was so moved by the story that he wrote an article about it. Dutch publishers read the article and immediately took an interest in the diary. On June 25, 1947, Anne's diary, titled *Het Achterhuis* (The Secret Annex), first appeared in print in the Netherlands.

For Otto, the publication was bittersweet. The book would bring Anne's experience into the hearts and minds of readers, but it would not bring his daughter back to life.

After the war, the Dutch government tried to identify those who had betrayed Jews in hiding. Willem van Maaren, Lammert Hartog, and Lammert's wife, Lena, all Opekta employees, came under investigation. All three had reason to believe Jews were hiding in the annex. Deliveries of large amounts of food to the office could have made them suspicious. They might also have noticed that the offices were used at night after the employees had left. Lena had even discussed the possibility of Jews hiding in the annex with Bep. She worried that if Jews were found there, she and her husband could be held responsible and arrested.

In March 1948, the Amsterdam police questioned the employees. But the investigation proved inconclusive, and the case was closed.

Anne wrote in her diary that she would make her voice heard. She wanted to go on living even after her death.

chapter 17

Anne's Greatest Wish

After the publication of *Het Achterhuis* in the Netherlands, an expanded version of the diary was published in several other countries. These editions included additional passages in which Anne spoke openly about her relationships with her family and the others in hiding.

Three notebooks were found: the red-checked diary Anne had been given as a thirteenth birthday present, a black notebook, and a notebook with a green-and-gold speckled cover. Anne had worked on revisions of her diary in hopes of having it published, and all

Anne Frank's diary has been translated into 52 languages (from Armenian and Nepali to Icelandic and Thai) and published in over 60 countries.

of these were preserved. In compiling the book for publication, Otto used passages from Anne's original diaries as well as ones from her revised manuscript.

Although in revising her diary Anne had chosen to omit some of the more emotional passages where she talks about her anger toward her mother, Otto reinstated some of these in his final version. Perhaps he wanted to give the reader a better understanding of the intensity of Anne's emotions. Otto made decisions about which version to use, but he did not change Anne's words—with one exception: In one passage Anne had referred to "the Germans"; Otto, however, did not want to condemn all Germans, and changed the wording to "these Germans."

In 1950, both French and German translations of Anne's diary were published. Barbara Mooyaart, a British woman living in the Netherlands and married to a Dutchman, was asked to do the English translation. She was deeply moved by the book, had a good grasp of the Dutch language, and could also understand the mind of a teenager. Her translation, *Anne Frank: The Diary of a Young Girl*, was published in the United States and Great Britain in 1952. After its publication, the editor of the book, Barbara Zimmerman, wrote to Otto to tell him about the excellent reviews the book had received in *The New York Times*, *The New York Herald Tribune*, and *Time* magazine.

In her letter she added these words: "It is extremely gratifying for me to work on the book because I believe so strongly in it.

Besides my great feeling for it, I believe it to be one of the very important diaries of all time, as a psychological, historical, and a literary document."

The decision to publish the diary had been a difficult one for Otto. But he knew he was helping to make Anne's greatest wish come true. What he didn't know yet was that over the years her book would be published in more than 50 languages and read around the world.

Otto had lost both his daughters, but he kept in touch with their school friends who had survived the war. Hanneli Goslar was one of them. Just before Bergen-Belsen was liberated, Hanneli and other prisoners were forced to march to a train stop, where they were put on cattle cars to be transported to the Theresienstadt concentration camp. On April 23, 1945, Russian soldiers liberated the train. Hanneli was suffering from typhus and was sent by the Red Cross to a hospital in Maastricht. When Otto heard that Hanneli was there, he made the 100-mile journey to see her, much of it by foot. Hanneli remembers that Otto was overjoyed to see her, but at the

Otto wanted to live "with" the past, but not "in" it. He kept Anne's memory alive and embraced people from all races, religions, and walks of life.

same time she could hear his heart crying, "Why didn't my Anne come back, too?"

On the train leaving Auschwitz, Otto had met another of Anne's school friends, Eva Geiringer. Eva introduced him to her mother, Fritzi, and the three spoke briefly. After returning to Amsterdam, Otto frequently saw Fritzi and Eva, and shared with them parts of Anne's diary before it was published. Otto was broken-hearted when he first visited them, but as time passed he worked hard to overcome his grief. He took comfort in being with Eva, who was the same age Anne would have been if she had lived. Otto also found he had much in common with Fritzi, who had lost both her husband and son during the war.

Otto captured Fritzi's heart with his charm and tremendous energy. Several years later, on November 10, 1953, the two were married at the city hall in Amsterdam. Miep and Jan Gies and the Kleimans attended. Otto and Fritzi then settled in Basel, Switzerland, close to Otto's sister and her family.

Anne's sharp eye, her gift of analysis, and her desire to improve herself and make the world a more peaceful place made a deep impression on Otto. He wanted to bring Anne's message to the world, to tell young people to work for peace and understanding, and to encourage people of different religions to work together.

"It is one of the very important diaries of all time."

Barbara Zimmerman

Readers of *The Diary of a Young Girl* were often so moved that they wrote to Otto to tell him how they identified with Anne's struggles and her strong desire to do something important with her life. They saw in Otto a father or friend in whom they could confide. Some sought advice on how to find happiness or asked for help in making decisions. Others simply wanted to share with Otto how much the book had touched them.

Letters seeking advice or a comforting word from Otto came from the Netherlands, the United States, Japan, Germany, and many other countries. Many of those who wrote to Otto had suffered greatly during the war, but found in Anne's story much-needed inspiration. The diary gave them hope and helped them face the future. Other young readers, born after the war, could also see themselves in Anne. Some felt they knew Anne better than anyone else they had ever met.

Through the years several attacks on the authenticity of Anne's diary were made. But efforts to prove that Anne had written the diary, including analysis of Anne's handwriting, were all successful. In 1989, the publication of *The Diary of Anne Frank: The Critical Edition*, by the Netherlands State Institute for War Documentation, which had kept Anne's original writings, confirmed once again that the diary was written by Anne Frank. This book also made it possible for the public to examine the three versions of the diary: Version A, Anne's original diary;

Anne's Story on the Stage

For the stage adaptation of *The Diary of Anne Frank*, Otto decided against playwright Meyer Levin, whose script focused on Anne's Jewish heritage, and chose Hollywood writers Frances Goodrich and Albert Hackett instead. The play opened in New York on October 5, 1955, and won the Pulitzer Prize for drama. Otto, however, could not fully enjoy its success—Levin's disappointment in not being chosen resulted in a painful legal battle.

Version B, Anne's revised diary; and Version C, the diary that was first published with passages Otto selected from the original and revised diaries.

In the 30 years following the publication of the diary, Otto received 30,000 letters from readers. Fritzi recognized Otto's wonderful gift for reaching out to young people and helped him answer each letter personally. Together they devoted four hours a day to letter writing.

To his youngest correspondents, Otto tried to explain in simple terms that they must not regard one race or religion as better or worse than another. That Anne had wanted to make her voice heard, just as they could. That wars would never solve the problems of the world. And that all people, politicians and ordinary citizens, must work to end discrimination.

chapter 18

Anne's Legacy

In 1956, Otto learned that the offices and annex at 263 Prinsengracht were about to be torn down. Otto and other concerned citizens raised money to stop the demolition. They not only succeeded in preserving the building, but also made plans to open the "Anne Frank House" to the public. The group founded the Anne Frank Youth Center to teach young people about prejudice and discrimination.

Otto shows Queen Juliana of the Netherlands the swinging bookcase in the secret annex. The queen visited the annex on June 12, 1979, the fiftieth anniversary of Anne's birth.

The Anne Frank House opened its doors in 1960. Visitors could walk through the Opekta offices

The Franks' hiding place is now open to the public. Every year more than 900,000 people from all over the world come to visit. The Anne Frank House museum also organizes educational programs to encourage people to fight discrimination and promote tolerance.

where Otto, Mr. van Pels, and the helpers had worked.

They could also see the swinging bookcase, climb the steep stairs, and discover the rooms where Anne and the others had lived. These rooms were kept much the way they were in 1945—the blacked-out windows, the same yellow wallpaper. Anne's photographs of movie stars and royalty were still pasted on the walls of the room she shared first with Margot and then with Dr. Pfeffer. Believing that everyone could benefit from the experience, Otto encouraged Jews and non-Jews, Germans and non-Germans, to visit the Anne Frank House.

Otto was the only resident of the secret annex to return to Amsterdam. None of the others survived the concentration camps—they would never read Anne's diary nor visit the annex. In late October or early November 1944, Hermann van Pels, imprisoned at Auschwitz, was sent to the gas chambers. Auguste van Pels, who had been at Bergen-Belsen with Anne and Margot, was transported to Buchenwald in Germany, and, on April 9, 1945, to Theresienstadt in Czechoslovakia. The exact date of her death is unknown.

Peter died at Mauthausen in Austria on May 5, 1945, three days before U.S. soldiers liberated the camp. Fritz Pfeffer was sent to the Neuengamme concentration camp in Germany and died there on December 20, 1944. He was survived by his fiancée, Charlotte Kaletta, as well as a son, Werner Pfeffer, who had escaped to London before the war and later emigrated to California.

At home in Basel, Switzerland, Otto and Fritzi formed the ANNE FRANK-Fonds (Anne Frank Foundation) to support charitable work. This organization was dedicated to promoting better understanding between different religions, serving the cause of peace, and encouraging exchange

Otto visits children in Düsseldorf where a new school, the Anne Frank School, would be built. Otto shared his belief that it is everyone's responsibility to fight prejudice.

programs between young people from different countries.

Otto did not forget the constant care, the many acts of kindness, and the moral support the helpers provided. He nominated Miep and Jan Gies, Bep Voskuijl, Victor Kugler, and Johannes Kleiman for medals of honor, awarded by the Commission for the Righteous in Jerusalem in 1973. In his letter of recommendation, Otto stated that they were well aware of the dangerous task they had undertaken in helping the Jews—they had risked imprisonment, deportation, and death.

Even when he was well into his eighties, Otto enjoyed being around young people. In their presence, he said he could forget that he was old and be one of them. Otto also remained interested in politics and education. Once a month, he traveled to Amsterdam to promote the work of the Anne Frank House. He wanted to keep alive the memory of all those who suffered during World War II so that the world would learn from history. Both Otto and Fritzi also frequently visited Eva, her husband, and their three daughters in England. They adored the children and took great delight in being grandparents.

Otto kept up his correspondence and his work with the ANNE FRANK-Fonds until his death from lung cancer, at the age of 91, on August 19, 1980. Memorial services were held in Basel and New York the following October. Friends of Otto's and Anne's came from afar to offer tributes, and Otto's favorite poems and prayers were read. One offers a plea that those who have died be remembered by the good they have done and the truth they have spoken.

Today Bernd "Buddy" Elias, Anne's first cousin, who played with Anne as a child, runs the ANNE FRANK-Fonds in Basel. The foundation, along with the Anne Frank House, continues to support the work Otto started—to combat all forms of racism and anti-Semitism and to spread Anne's message to the world. Buddy says to himself almost every day, "Anne, if only you knew what became of your diary."

In 1987 Miep, together with author Alison Leslie Gold, wrote a memoir titled *Anne Frank Remembered*. Miep tells her own story as well as Anne's. She talks about life inside the annex, as well as the world beyond its walls, the world Anne was not allowed to see. She describes the difficulties in finding food, the wartime conditions, the risks taken by Jews and non-Jews. Miep makes it clear that she never wanted to claim credit for what she had done. She was fond of saying, "You do what you have to do." And she would add that the real heroes were the people in hiding.

Miep Gies holds a copy of her book, *Anne Frank Remembered*. Miep believes it is important for younger generations to remember Anne so that her voice and her legacy will never be lost.

Anne's diary tells the story of a young girl with a temper that was difficult to control. As a schoolgirl, she was pretty, lively, fun-loving, and adventurous. But, once confined to the annex, she turned inward. Her life became something frightening and intense. Her experience was extraordinary, yet her feelings and emotions are familiar to everyone. Anne could be angry, jealous, or selfish—she could also be joyful, passionate, and eager to reach out to others.

She tried to look beyond herself, seeking to better the world and to promote peace and understanding among people of different races and religion. She wanted so much to be a writer. In that, she succeeded. She shared with her readers keen insights and funny moments, her dreams and her despair, her frequent vexations and her great capacity for love.

Those who survived—Otto, Fritzi, Miep, Buddy, and others—have helped deliver Anne's message to the world. Almost 20 million copies of Anne's diary have been printed, and Anne's voice has been heard around the world. Anne has become a symbol of the murder of six million Jews—and of all those who have been subject to persecution. She is also a symbol of faith and courage. Otto missed his daughter terribly, but he knew she was living in the hearts of many people.

Anne's death reminds us of the suffering and cruelty we cannot escape. Her life reminds us that we can try.

Events in the Life of Anne Frank

June 12, 1929
Annelies Marie Frank is
born in Frankfurt.

November 9, 1938
Nazis attack Jewish homes and
businesses during Kristallnacht
(Night of Broken Glass).

May 12, 1925
Edith Holländer and
Otto Frank are married
in Aachen, Germany.

September 1, 1939
The German invasion
of Poland marks the
start of World War II.

February 22, 1941
The Nazis begin the
first roundup of the
Jews in Amsterdam.

1925

Autumn 1933
The Franks move to
Amsterdam to
escape anti-Semitism
in Germany.

May 15, 1940
The Netherlands
surrenders after
the German
invasion.

June 12, 1942
Anne makes the
first entry in her
diary on her
13th birthday.

January 30, 1933
Adolf Hitler is
appointed chancellor
of Germany.

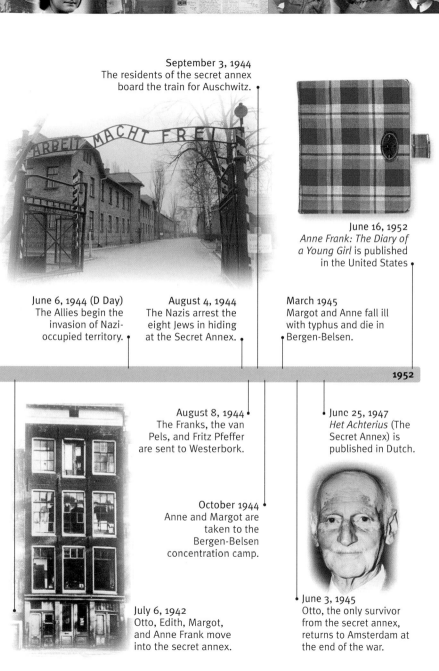

September 3, 1944
The residents of the secret annex board the train for Auschwitz.

June 16, 1952
Anne Frank: The Diary of a Young Girl is published in the United States

June 6, 1944 (D Day)
The Allies begin the invasion of Nazi-occupied territory.

August 4, 1944
The Nazis arrest the eight Jews in hiding at the Secret Annex.

March 1945
Margot and Anne fall ill with typhus and die in Bergen-Belsen.

1952

August 8, 1944
The Franks, the van Pels, and Fritz Pfeffer are sent to Westerbork.

June 25, 1947
Het Achterius (The Secret Annex) is published in Dutch.

October 1944
Anne and Margot are taken to the Bergen-Belsen concentration camp.

July 6, 1942
Otto, Edith, Margot, and Anne Frank move into the secret annex.

June 3, 1945
Otto, the only survivor from the secret annex, returns to Amsterdam at the end of the war.

Sources

Books:

Anne Frank House: A Museum with a Story. Amsterdam: Anne Frank Stichting, 2001.

Bachrach, Susan D. *Tell Them We Remember: The Story of the Holocaust.* Boston: Little, Brown and Company, 1994.

Frank, Anne. *Anne Frank The Diary of a Young Girl,* translated by B. M. Mooyart. Doubleday. New York: Doubleday, 1952.

Frank, Anne. *The Diary of a Young Girl: The Definitive Edition,* edited by Otto H. Frank & Mirjam Pressler, translated by Susan Massotty. New York: Doubleday, 1995.

Frank, Anne. *Tales from the Secret Annex,* translated by Michael Mok. New York: Doubleday, 1984.

Gies, Miep, and Alice Leslie Gold. *Anne Frank Remembered: The Story of the Woman Who Helped to Hide the Frank Family.* New York: Simon and Schuster, 1987.

Gold, Alice Leslie. *Memories of Anne Frank: Reflections of a Childhood Friend.* New York: Scholastic, 1997.

Greenfield, Howard. *The Hidden Children.* New York: Ticknor and Fields, 1993.

Het Verzetsmuseum Amsterdam/The Dutch Resistance Museum. Amsterdam: Verzetsmuseum, 2000.

Lee, Carol Ann. *The Hidden Life of Otto Frank.* New York: HarperCollins, 2003.

Lindwer, Willy. *The Last Seven Months of Anne Frank.* New York: Anchor Books, 1992.

Meltzer, Milton. *Never to Forget: The Jews of the Holocaust.* New York: Harper Collins, 1976.

Müller, Melissa. *Anne Frank [The Biography].* New York: Henry Holt, 1999.

Schloss, Eva. *Eva's Story: A Survivor's Tale by the Step Sister of Anne Frank.* London: W.H. Allen, 1988.

Schnabel, Ernst. *Anne Frank: A Portrait in Courage.* New York: Harcourt Brace, 1958.

van der Rol, Ruud, and Rian Verhoeven. *Anne Frank: Beyond the Diary.* New York: Viking, 1993.

van Maarsen, Jacqueline. *My Friend Anne Frank.* New York: Vantage Press, 1996.

Articles and Essays:

Brilliant, Moshe. "Anne Frank's Friend." *The New York Times Magazine.* April 21, 1957: 30–32.

Kugler, Victor. "The Reminiscences of Victor Kugler." (told to Eda Shapiro). *Yad Vashem Studies XIII.* Jerusalem, 1979: 358–383.

Metselaar, Menno. "The Day Before Going into Hiding." *Anne Frank Magazine* 1999: 14–17.

Metselaar, Menno. "A Margot Frank House? The Forgotten Sister of Anne Frank." *Anne Frank Magazine* 2000: 28–35.

Nieman, John. "Otto Frank Revisited." *Israel Today.* June 6, 1979: 6–7.

Nussbaum, Laureen. "Anne Frank." in *Anne Frank: Reflections on Her Life and Legacy,* edited by Hyman Aaron Enzer and Sandra Solotaroff-Enzer. Urbana: University of Illinois Press, 2000.

Paape, Harry. "The Arrest." in *The Diary of Anne Frank: The Critical Edition.* New York: Doubleday, 1989.

Pick, Lies Goslar, as told to Stanley Frank. "I Knew Anne Frank." *McCalls* July 1958: 30.

Pratt, Jane. "The Anne Frank We Remember." *McCalls* Jan. 1986: 72+.

Schnabel, Ernst. "What Happened after Anne Frank's Diary." *Life.* Aug. 18, 1958: 78–90.

Trappen, Michelle. "Life and Death." *Sunday Oregonian.* Oct. 4, 1992: L1+.

Unger, Arthur. "Anne Frank and her Sheltering Friends." *Christian Science Monitor.* April 14, 1988: 21–22.

Citations:

"God knows everything..." on p. 19: *The Last Seven Months of Anne Frank* p. 17.

"My wife and I did our best..." on p. 25: Otto Frank's memorandum.

"Miep, where seven can eat..." on p. 40: *Anne Frank Remembered* p. 133.

"Yes, Miep, as you know..." on p. 54: "Anne Frank and Her Sheltering Friends" p. 21

"capacity of observing which was astonishing" on p. 54: Otto Frank's memorandum.

"You know how often we share some secret..." on p. 58: Letter from Otto Frank to Anne, May 12, 1939, translated by J.W.F. Stoppelman.

"We can start now..." on p. 79: Anne Frank's Tales from the Secret Annex p. 131.

"Caught with them..." on p. 84: "The Reminiscences of Victor Kugler" p. 360.

"It was summer outside..." on p. 85: "What Happened after Anne Frank's Diary" p. 80.

"Auschwitz was really the end..." on p.89: *The Last Seven Months of Anne Frank* p. 156.

"You cannot imagine..." on p. 92: *Anne Frank: A Portrait in Courage* p. 169.

"I never stop thinking about them." on p. 104: Letter from Otto Frank to his mother, June 8, 1945.

"Here is your daughter Anne's legacy..." on p. 105: *Anne Frank Remembered* p. 235.

"It is extremely gratifying..." on p. 111: Letter from Barbara Zimmerman to Otto Frank, June 12, 1952.

"Why didn't my Anne..." on p. 112: "I Knew Anne Frank" p. 114.

"Anne, if only you knew..." on p. 120: from "Remarks by Bernd 'Buddy' Elias" at the opening of "Anne Frank the Writer" exhibit at the U. S. Holocaust Memorial Museum, June 11, 2003.

Author's note

I am most grateful to Rene Blekman, Erika Prins, Karolien Stocking, and Yt Stoker at the Anne Frank House in Amsterdam for providing their assistance as well as giving me the opportunity to read materials in their collection, including numerous newspaper clippings, unpublished letters, and documents. Many thanks to Dr. Erik Somers for reading the finished manuscript and offering such good advice and counsel. I also wish to thank the ANNE FRANK–Fonds in Basel, especially Buddy Elias and Peter M. Loewe, for their kind permission to quote from the archives. The United States Holocaust Memorial Museum library staff graciously assisted me in my research. Beth Hester's careful editing, clear vision, and good sense made this book possible. Special thanks also go to my husband Jon and to my family. This book is for you.

For Further Study Visit

The **United States Holocaust Memorial Museum** in Washington, D.C. (www.ushmm.org) tells the story of the Holocaust and the six million people who were killed.

The **Secret Annex at the Anne Frank House** in Amsterdam (www.annefrank.nl) is just as the Franks left it. Visitors can also see museum exhibits related to ending discrimination and promoting tolerance.

Index

Picture Credits